Herbert Brase

My Ministry In Canada:

As I Remember It

Published by Mercinator Press

mercinatorpress@gmail.com

14205 Ida St.
Omaha NE 68142

First edition: 1975
Second edition 2019

Herbert Brase.
My Ministry In Canada
As I Remember It
Mercinator Press
ISBN: 978-0-9975197-5-4

Foreword

Dear Reader: In this book you have the story of the incidents or experiences in the twenty-one years of my life as a minister of the Lord God in Northwest Saskatchewan, Canada. As you read the book, I would like for you to imagine that you and I are sitting comfortably in an easy chair in my or your home, sipping a cup of tea or coffee or whatever you wish, and I am telling you about my life as a missionary-pastor while in Canada just as it comes to my mind. The facts I am telling you are true, but not always in chronological order. Therefore the book is not divided into chapters with specific headings. I do hope that you will enjoy reading it.

I have several purposes for writing this book:

1. That Christians may know what their missionaries in foreign countries go through, do, and endure;

2. That Christians may become more mission-minded;

3. That Christians be moved to become more liberal in their prayers and offerings for our missions in all the world; if this book brings this about. I shall be amply rewarded for time and effort put into the writing of it; and

4. The chief purpose of this book, however, is to give glory, not to myself, but to God alone, who has so graciously and lovingly protected me, guided and truly blessed my efforts and work done for Him and His kingdom of grace.

It is God who sent me into Northwest Saskatchewan. I was His instrument in His hands to cast out the Seed, but He gave the increase. The fruit of my labors was His doing and is a proof of the truth of His word and promise that His word shall not return unto Him void. (Isaiah 55:11) It also proves that He keeps His promise to go with us even to the ends of the earth and that He will never leave nor forsake His people and that He gives His angels charge over them to keep them in all their ways as they walk according to His word, doing His will. Glory be to God! And may He bring about the fulfilment of the purposes of this book.

Ash Wednesday, February 12, 1975.

Dedication

I DEDICATE THIS BOOK to my loving and faithful wife, Hildegard, who, under God, has helped to make my ministry the success it was and who was a most efficient and true mother to our five girls and brought them up in the fear of the Lord. I also dedicate this book to our five girls: Delilah, a parochial schoolteacher in Faribault, Minnesota; Vera May, formerly a laboratory technician and a faithful church worker in Lloydminster, Alberta; Aleta, a clerk at her husband's auction sales and active in the church near Omaha, Nebraska; Cordelia, who is serving and praising God in glory; and Lois, a secretary and also faithful to her Lord and church in Oklahoma City, Oklahoma.

Also do I warmly and sincerely and most tastefully acknowledge the help so freely given by Mrs. Lola Schultze in the typing of the original manuscript and by my daughter, Lois, in the typing of the final copy.

Preface

When Dr. Fritz, Dean at the Seminary in St. Louis, Missouri, wanted an interview with a student, he would send a card to the student's room. The card would tell the student when he was to report to the Dean's office. The code on the card would tell the Dean for what purpose he wanted to interview the student. This could be good; it could be bad. One day I received a card. I reported at the appointed time. He wanted to know whether I could speak German. I could. He asked about my home and parents and whether I had a girl friend. We, however, were not allowed to be engaged before graduation. But he wanted to know whether I would have a wife to take along if I were called to serve in some foreign mission field. My computer must have been so stunned at the question that it did not record my answer because there is nothing in my memory as to the answer I gave him. I was engaged at the time; however, I did not reveal that fact to the Dean. I could not take the chance. That was the interview.

A few months later the calls were issued. I received a call to Rock Haven, Saskatchewan, Canada. I informed the girl I had asked to marry me and she readily expressed her willingness to go with me. I am glad I did not tell her mama first because she was not so keen on that idea which took her firstborn out of the country to a foreign land far away. I did not relay the good news of the willingness of the girl I had asked to go with me to the Dean. I had good reasons for keeping it secret. Graduation had not yet taken place but was only a few days off. And when that great day was at hand, so were my bride-to-be, my parents, and my oldest brother. A few days after graduation we were home in Worms, Nebraska. Here busy days were ahead of us getting the wedding plans for the 30th of July, 1930, into good working order and likewise securely packing all the nice things we were taking with us to our first home in Canada, the beautiful land north of the border, after a short honeymoon, part of which we spent in the Nebraska State Penitentiary in Lincoln. No, not for the reason you may be thinking, dear Reader, but just to visit. That was different and unusual for a honeymoon. Agreed? Wonder if any other couple ever did anything like that on their honeymoon. I believe that distinction belongs to us alone.

About the middle of August we were ready to leave for Canada in my $45.00 Model T coupe. My father built a "house" on the back of my Model T which made it look as though I might be a "Rawleigh's Medicine" peddler. We packed the things we were taking to Canada with us into that "house" and it was packed full and tight. A day or two before leaving for Canada, my classmate, who was also my roommate for two years at the Seminary, arrived in his Model T sedan with his bride and the back seat packed full. They were from Sedalia, Missouri. He also had a call to Saskatchewan. The night before we left Worms for our long journey to the land north of the border, we had a "crackin' good" electric storm and a heavy downpour of rain.

The next morning the two preachers, with their brides and what-have-you, headed their Model T's north. Our trail took us through the famous sand hills of Nebraska where the roads are so winding that at times we could see the back end of our Model T's as we went around the bends — well, almost. In South Dakota we drove through the Black Hills where we went sight-seeing for a while and also visited a friend or relative of the Fellwocks. They were our traveling partners. We stayed one night with them, if my memory is not playing tricks on me as I write this. The next day we had prairie trails in the cattle country (Marlboro country) in Montana. Skipping along on those smooth trails, a big bull, like a fat policeman, stood right in the trail. We did not stop to ask questions or argue with him but politely tipped out hats and turned off the trail and whizzed by him. A wise move, wouldn't you say?

Eventually, probably the second day after the Black Hills and the "bullish" roadblock in Montana, we arrived at the Canadian border where we had to stop and report to the custom's officer. He was a young man substituting for the regular officer who was on holiday, as they say in Canada. This young man was rather puzzled about what to do regarding my Model T which cost me only $45.00. He just would not believe me, even after I showed him my papers, and he was not inclined to enter that cost or price on the official paper. Everything else we had we could take in duty-free under "settler's effects." This I knew. I had informed myself beforehand. He kept us there quite a while during which time he was searching in books to learn just what he should do. We were not too happy with the delay because of his ignorance. Finally, he must have sensed this and then said that he would ask the regular officer when he returned and if there was anything to be done about it, he would write to me. He never did write to me, which I knew he would not from the information I had gotten before I ever left home. We wanted to get to Regina yet that day and it was late afternoon already. Regina is the capital of Saskatchewan.

Once more on the way, we had about two hundred miles to go to get to Regina. It was dark before we arrived there but we could see the lights of Regina probably twenty or thirty miles away. They seemed so close, but it seemed like an eternity to get there. Finally, four tired people, foreigners, arrived in the capital city of big Saskatchewan. It was about ten o'clock. Where do we stay for the night and where do we eat? We saw a sign: "Hotel Saskatchewan." We went there. A "ritzy" place. Should we poor Yankee preachers go in there? I must have been so tired that my memory machine did not record whether we did or not. I can say, however, that we did stay in Regina our first night in a country that I, in time, learned to love and still do.

Morning came just like it does in the States. After our first breakfast in Canada, we headed north some more, about forty miles, where we stopped in Southy to call on the Lutheran pastor there. Here we spent a day and a night getting information from the pastor. And this was also the point of the parting-of-ways for the Fellwocks and the Brases. The Fellwocks headed east possibly six or ten miles to Markinch, the parish to which he was called. My pretty bride and I headed northwest some more, about four hundred miles, to Rock Haven, the parish to which we were called. Rock Haven was only a small village about thirty-five miles southwest of North Battleford.

Under God's gracious guidance and protection, we arrived safely in our Model T which resembled a Rawleigh Medicine Peddler's outfit. Some people told us later that that is what they thought we were when we arrived. We inquired about the Lutheran church parsonage. We found it and some members working at remodeling an old house into a parsonage.

Not being completed enough to be livable, we stayed a night or two with a member out in the country a few miles. We arrived the week of August 24, 1930, possibly Wednesday of that week which was the 27th.

Whereas the parsonage was not completed, a summer cottage was rented for us to live in for the time being. The town water system was close by. It was a deep hole in the ground. The "old oaken bucket" was hanging on a long rope on the well. All that was necessary to get a drink of cold, fresh water was to let the bucket down and when filled, pull it up again. And should you find a mouse or something bigger swimming in the water, just fish it out and take it home. No, not the mouse or something bigger, but the water which you have transferred to a pail you brought with you. Then enjoy a drink of cold, fresh water. I wonder if the Jews and Samaritans drew up mice or something bigger out of Jacob's well near Sychar? If so, did they do as we did in Rock Haven? Why do you suppose they called the village "Rock Haven"? You guessed it. And now that your thirst is well quenched, I shall lead you into my story of:

MY MINISTRY IN CANADA
"AS I REMEMBER IT"

My Ministry In Canada: "As I Remember It"

On Sunday, August 31st, 1930, I was ordained and installed into the office of the holy ministry of God's Word and the Sacraments by the Rev. William Reitz, Field Secretary of the Manitoba-Saskatchewan District of The Lutheran Church-Missouri Synod. Saturday night it turned cold — cold enough to freeze ice. The wheat crop was quite late because a hail storm on July 1st had cut the wheat down but the farmers reseeded at such a late date. The wheat was short but looked good and was headed out. It was still green. It was cold all day Sunday — brrr! My bride and I are native Nebraskans and our Nebraska-weather clothes did not keep our thin blood warm. And I, a new young preacher, fresh out of the factory, just being ordained and installed, wished so hard, of all things: that the preacher would say "Amen" to his "long" sermon so that I could go down into the warm basement from which the aroma of that coffee — "Butter-Nut?" hardly; nor "Folgers, mountain grown, the richest kind" — was entering my nostrils urging me to follow the scent and find warmth and comfort. I never was so glad to hear the "Amen" when Rev. Reitz finally said it. I wonder how many times people were glad when they heard me say the "Amen" of my sermons. When the time came for me to make my ordination and installation vow, my vocal chords seemed to be frozen. But after some effort I was able to make my vow to which, by the grace of God, I have remained true to this day.

After a noon lunch and hot coffee I felt very comfortable and would have liked to stay there. The Rev. Reitz, however, insisted that I go with him; in fact, take him in my Model T to Spy Ridge, a preaching station of the Leipzig parish, where he would conduct a worship service. The pastor of this parish was on sick leave in the United States. The Mission Board of the District asked me to serve that parish in addition to my own while that pastor was on sick leave.

If there had been instant coffee in those days, there would have been no coffee aroma to distract me. But there was no instant coffee then. Neither was there a Lutheran church building in Rock Haven, nor anywhere else in my parish of three preaching stations: Rock Haven, Thackery, and Baldwinton. In Rock Haven we rented the United Church of Canada church building. At the other places we used public school buildings or the homes of members for worship services. My assignments were to increase the membership and also begin new preaching stations. This was not easy in a sparsely settled area and where the United Church of Canada counted everyone who signed their guest book as their member. The United Church of Canada was a very liberal and ecumenical organization, a union of the Congregational and the Methodist churches and the lax and liberal Presbyterians. In various places they simply took possession of the Presbyterian church buildings. The few good and conservative Presbyterians then had to relocate and rebuild.

Many of the pastors of the United Church denied the fundamental doctrines of the Bible. I know of one pastor who in a Bible Class was asked whether Jesus is the Son of God and he replied: "I don't know and I don't care." Another was told by a Lutheran lady that she was not attending his church any longer because he was not preaching the truth of the Bible. His reply was: "My dear lady, I know that. If I did preach what I should, I would lose many of my members." She came to my church after I started one in her town and she told me this. Another pastor asked the young people to answer this question in writing: "What would I like most to be?" and he would use their answers for his sermon. He had an article in the newspaper telling about it. An easy way get a sermon ready, I thought. I must hear that sermon! He had evening services so one of my young men and I went to hear that sermon. The first thing he said was that he did not receive a single reply, but that he would answer the question anyway. He spoke for at least 30 minutes and not one word about sin, repentance, faith, salvation, nor was the name Jesus or Christ spoken even once; only the name God once when he was quoting a poem. And he never did give us an answer to the question he promised to answer. I never did find out what he would like most of all to be, but I did find out what he was not.

Another thing that made my assignment difficult was the fact that at the very beginning of my ministry I had to serve, as I already mentioned, another parish, the pastor of which was on sick leave. It was a parish of one organized congregation in Leipzig, about 60 miles south, and three or four preaching stations. The parsonage at Rock Haven not being ready, the parish rented a summer cottage for us to live in temporarily. The men working at the parsonage were invited by my kind wife to eat their noon meal with us, which they did. One of these meals was a most embarrassing occasion for both them and us. The pie crust was as hard as plywood — well, almost. The men really had to bear down to get a bite. But it all came out all right, was soon forgotten, and there were no ill aftereffects. Where is the woman who does not have at least one tough pie crust in her life?

While living in the summer cottage we had a howling but cold initiation which lasted three days, October 15, 16, and 17. It was the worst blizzard during our 21 years in Canada. To keep reasonably warm, we burned our crating and boxes the first day. But they did not last and we had nothing else to burn. And the cook stove was the only stove we had. So I made my way against the wind and snow to a coal dealer who lived right next to the parsonage. A jolly good Scotchman, but not "scotch." His place of business, however, was at least a third of a mile away. I took a gunny sack to carry some coal home. On my way my eyes were covered with ice. I ran into a huge snow bank. I could see only a few feet ahead. I threw myself down and rolled to the left. Why I did that I don't know except that God was protecting me. I rolled off the end of the bank, got up, and close by there was a little shed of some kind with the door partly open and banging in the wind. I went in there to get the snow and ice off my face and eyes and to catch my breath. Then I proceeded to the coal dealer and made it there. He called me a few names for being so insane to think he would give me some coal. He flatly refused to sell me any coal and let me carry it home. "That would be murder," he said, "and I will not take that upon my conscience." I then asked him to have the drayman bring me some. "The drayman," he said, "refused to go out in this weather because he can not see where he is going. He tried it yesterday but had to give up." Oh, it was a humdinger, that blizzard! Well, all I could do was take my gunny sack and carry it back home the way I brought it — empty! But it was better going back home with the wind.

My next door neighbor, a typical Englishman, the butcher in town, had three big lumps of coal left from the winter before, and he threw one over the fence for me to have. Now we could get some warmth into our summer cottage. But oh, when we did, the ceiling began to leak here and there. The attic was packed with snow! Oh, what an initiation to Canadian winter weather!

Most of the late wheat crop was under the snow and a loss. Our house was almost completely surrounded by a huge drift. But it warmed up again and all the snow, except for some of the huge drifts, disappeared. For the remainder of our first winter in Canada we had about 3 inches of snow and the weather was unusually mild.

We moved into the parsonage the early part of November. It was small, but nice and comfortable. Ample room for the two of us and even for my classmate and his bride, the Langbeckers, when they came to visit us from North Battleford, about 35 miles northeast of Rock Haven where they were called to serve the Lord and His church.

At Baldwinton, northwest of Rock Haven about 25 miles, I had nothing unusual in my very first service, except very few people. One family had two boys to instruct for confirmation. This I did in their home and I also went there during the week between services for instruction. Then I stayed overnight with them. They, too, as so many, were poor people. I slept in the same room with their daughters, due to lack of room. My bed had wooden slats with a straw mattress on them — no springs. The slats would not always "stay put" all night long. Kabang, there goes one! Maybe later another. What position was I in by now?!

The woman of the house was the man's second wife. The boys I was instructing for confirmation were his. He got his second wife by placing an ad in the newspaper. It was answered by a woman from California. She was a member of the Four Square Gospel or the Pentecostal church. It makes little difference which — they are the same flavor. They got acquainted by correspondence and snapshots. He sent for her, met her at the U.S. border, married her, and brought her home with him.

She soon ruled the roost, especially in religion. She made things difficult for him. Also for me. When I was there for the instruction of his boys, she, having gone to bed right after supper, would call out from the bedroom: "That is not true" and would keep on trying to correct me. Her husband felt very bad about it. She disturbed my class frequently and made it practically impossible. She also told me not to come back. However, I did try again to continue with the boys. She had her husband going to a Pentecostal church in the community by this time. He was leaning in that direction.

He wanted me to go along and see for myself that they were all right. One Sunday when I was there for our service held in a school house, if I remember correctly, they were not in my church service that afternoon. I went to their home for instruction of the boys, but had none. There was a Pentecostal church service that evening and the boys and husband had to go there. He tried to excuse himself to me and also to persuade me to go along and see for myself. I did go and I did see for myself; I also heard for myself. He sat quite to the back. She and the rest of the family sat quite to the front. They sang and sang to music almost like a polka. Then the preacher prayed and prayed and the people shouted "Amen!" "Glory!" "Hallelujah! Praise the Lord!" Then some would testify. After this they would sing again, several hymns, swing music. Then the preacher would preach and he would shout, jump up on a chair, down again; he would work up a real sweat, take off his coat, preach and prance back and forth on the stage until he was out of breath. Then he would get them to sing some more, thus constantly working on the nerves of the people. Then an offering, more testifying, and more "Hallelujah!" "Glory be!" "Praise the Lord!" The preacher would then ask people to come to the front, get down on the floor and give themselves over to the Holy Spirit. Soon a few went to the front. The preacher went up and down the aisle to induce people. My member had gone out by now. There were quite a number lying on the floor groaning and moaning. This went on for some time — 20 to 30 minutes. It sounded pitiful. And it was!! By now my man was back in. The revival was almost over. Some began leaving. So did we. Yes. I saw for myself and heard for myself. I talked to the father but saw that there was no use that I continue coming for instructions. In the course of time we moved the place of service to a country school house west of Baldwinton several miles where we had a nice group attending — about 18 to 30 people. I instructed and confirmed several boys and a girl there.

At the same time I was also serving the Leipzig parish, the pastor of which was on sick leave in the U.S. Conducting services at Spy Ridge for the first time, I had an experience I still well remember and so does my bride. The people were German Russians. The service naturally was in

German. I picked the easiest and best-known hymns and melodies I knew. The first one was "Abide, O Dearest Jesus." There was no organist so I had to start them out and that is all I got done. They sang the hymn with all the many slurs they had in the old Volga Hymnal in Russia. I was in the second verse, second line, before they finished the first verse. So I just let them sing. Sliding around the way they did certainly lengthens the time of singing. The rest of the service was quite normal in order and procedure. The odd-style dress of the people, especially the women, was quite striking to me. And so was the way the men sat on top of the desks in the school house and rested their feet on the seats. The school teacher's desk was my altar, lectern, and pulpit. The way the women were dressed made my wife, with her "latest" from the U.S., feel quite conspicuous or out of place.

Serving Thackery, about 15 miles southeast of Rock Haven, I had an experience as a young preacher I can not forget. Either in my first or second worship service there, I was asked to confirm a lay-baptism which was performed by a Catholic lady who was the "nurse-maid" at the birth of a girl who was not expected to live. But she did. The nurse-maid called in two of the men who happened to be on the farmplace at the time and asked them to witness the baptism. These two gave witness of the baptism and that it was rightly performed according to Scripture; thus I confirmed the baptism and issued a certificate. The little girl grew up and became a real "go-getter" and most active in the Walther League for which she, no doubt, is still remembered.

Attendance at services was about 28 to 33 at Rock Haven, 10 to 40 at Baldwinton, 18 to 25 at Thackery. As time marched on, I began also English worship services at Thackery which resulted in raising the attendance from 35 to 50 people. Also, I began several more preaching stations with attendance from 10 to 25 souls. I instructed a few adults, some children, conducted Sunday Schools, made Mission calls, pastoral calls, sick calls, and constantly put more miles on my Model T which served me well. It was worth the $45.00 I had paid for it in 1929. It also took me back and forth from home in Nebraska to the seminary in St. Louis, 600 miles, several times. Also on a trip to sell Concordia Publishing House books and to visit my relatives in Oklahoma.

Some time before Christmas, the Leipzig pastor returned from sick leave, somewhat better, but not well. He offered to mimeograph the

Sunday School Christmas program for me. It was a cold day when my wife and I drove to Leipzig in our Model T. (Oh, I had removed the "thing" that gave the appearance of a Rawleigh Medicine peddler by this time.) After the mimeographing was completed and we visited over supper, we started on our way home. It was "brrr" cold. There was no anti-freeze for the radiator in those days. Somehow one tried do protect it from the wind with cardboard. But my aging Model T froze up and soon I had what looked like a steam engine. We got as far as Wilkie, about 30 miles from Rock Haven. There we had it thawed out and were on our way again. It was long after dark in Canada by now but not late at night. Again the radiator was frozen and began to leak. We stopped at a farm house for help. No one home. We tried the door; it was not locked. I had some matches (I had a "bad habit" in those days), lit one, found a lamp (farmers had no electric lights then), lit it. Oh, it was nice and warm in the house. I filled the radiator with warm water, covered it with a quilt we had with us, and left the engine running. The Mrs. was in the house where it was warm. I soon joined her. When all was thawed out, I added some more water and we were on our way again. About 10 or 15 miles from home our Model T "clunked out." It would not start again. Could hardly blame it in such cold weather. Don't remember how cold it was, but a ways below zero.

A short distance back we had passed a school house where there was a dance in progress. I walked back there — not to dance while my bride was snugly tucked away in the Model T, but to get help. Two young men said they were going to the dance in Rock Haven and that we could ride along. We then pushed our Model T off the road and were on our way home. They had a Ford Sedan. Model "A," I believe. Bottles of beer were rolling around on the floor. They drove, as one says, like crazy. There was some snow and the road or trail was winding. We were frightened and hung on for dear life and prayed that God would bring us safely home. He did, as He so often did while on mission trips.

The young men stopped at the dance hall. They would not take any pay, so we thanked them and walked to our new parsonage. The next day our good Scotch neighbor and I drove out and pulled my Model T home. All three of us were united again but one had to go to the "hospital" for repairs. Everything came out just fine and all were happy again.

It is now spring of 1931. The depression with its dust storms was in full swing, taking its toll, making progress in church work more difficult. The rich were not getting richer but the poor were getting poorer. Our starting salary was the huge sum of $85.00 per month. If I had not taken a wife, it would have been $80.00. What a great value was placed on a wife in those "good old days!" Salary that the various preaching stations pledged, but seldom paid in full, I had to report to the Board of Missions of the District as I received it during the year and the amount received was deducted from my salary check from the Board of Missions. I also had to report my mileage each month for which I received an allowance of 4¢ per mile, if I remember correctly. Collections at the services which I received — from 75¢ to $3.50 — were also to be reported and the amount was deducted from mileage allowance. The Board of Missions, however, placed a certain amount into a car fund for its missionaries for a car-replacement which the missionary could ask for when he needed it.

As I said above, the depression and dust storms were in full swing. The storms would last for days at a time, the dust sifting into the houses, even with storm windows on. Every 10 to 20 minutes we could write our names in the dust on the window sills. We would cover our dishes and food on the table with tea towels to keep the dust off.

One Sunday, driving in the dust storms to conduct services in two of the preaching stations in the Leipzig parish, I often could not see the radiator cap on my Model T when going with the wind. The dust was winning the race. I could not see the crossroads and finally decided I was lost. I came to a place where a farmer had planted some trees on his farm yard which broke the wind enough so I could see them and also the driveway. I turned in and asked for directions. The farmer told me I had gone two miles too far where I should have turned right. So I started back but against the wind my Model T really had to labor. Before long it was no longer hitting on all four because of dust that got into the coil box under the dash and was shorting out one, at times two, of them. Here is the corner where I now must turn left. Now I had the wind a little more behind me again. Only a short distance and there was the school house we used for a church. Only a few people were still there. The others had gone home again. I was quite late by now. I held an abbreviated worship service hoping I could get to the next school house before all those people would go home. I quickly ate the lunch my wife had made for me. It was flavored with dust even though in a paper bag. Then I took the coils into the school house, cleaned them, replaced them, and now all four were working again. It was important that a preacher also be a mechanic. (Possibly some of you reading this don't know what I am writing about: "coils, coil box under the dash." Ask Grandpa or maybe great-grandpa.) So I headed for the next school house but against the wind my Model T had a hard time. Often I had to use the low gear (it only had low and high) to get a little more speed so it would pull it on high.

On the way to the second school house, it began to drizzle. Before long I was in darkness, the windows being completely pasted over with mud except for a little space which I kept reasonably clean with a hand-operated windshield wiper. But the dust finally settled down; not the wind. When I got to the school house. I could see some buggy tracks in the wet dust. People had been there but had left again. I was really late by this time. So all that was left for me to do was to crank up my Model T and go home. I am thankful that such trips were only very occasional. At least 50 miles and I broke the Bread of Life to about five, maybe eight, people. But I recall that Jesus stopped to do that even for only one person. And He had no Model T to get from place to place. Wonder how often He walked in the wind and dust and rain and cold and heat?! And He did not have a place where to lay His head. How blessed we are even in our hardships: It felt good, believe me, to be at home again, out of the wind, eating a warm meal, and sleeping in a comfortable bed, even better than a straw mattress.

Rock Haven preaching station was in the process of writing a constitution to become an organized congregation, which they did under the name Immanuel Lutheran Church-Missouri Synod. But at the same time trouble was brewing in the congregation, mostly because I opposed our ladies joining in the "World Day of Prayer" with all the other denominations. This would involve our ladies in unionism which is contrary to God's will and Word. God wants unity and oneness in doctrine and in faith. However, other things were brought to my attention. One thing, the children had to memorize and study too much for confirmation. The Field Secretary, Rev. Reitz, visited me. He stayed overnight with one of the member families. There the plans apparently were laid to move me. The Field Secretary left again but returned later in the spring (1931). A second much-unexpected visit. He then informed me that the Board of Missions wanted me to become the missionary in the rich wheat-land area at Rosetown, about

130 miles south, on the prairie where one can see for miles in any direction. Rosetown was in the heart of this good wheat country.

Rock Haven, being now an organized congregation, asked for a definite candidate whom they knew and who would be graduated from the St. Louis Seminary in June. They got him.

The pastor of the Leipzig parish accepted a call to the U.S., southern Illinois. That meant that I again had that parish to serve as vacancy pastor.

The time for my removal from Rock Haven to Rosetown was near at hand. I confirmed all the children and adults whom I had in the instruction classes and brought my services to a close in the Rock Haven parish where I now had one more preaching station which was attended by about 25 and a Sunday School of 15 children. My final service was held in Rock Haven with the confirmation of eight children and the celebration of Holy Communion, August 9th, 1931.

The following Sunday I preached for a mission festival in Luseland, about 125 miles south. But before going there I took my wife to the hospital in North Battleford. While I was on my way to Luseland, Delilah Irene, our first-born, came to keep my wife company. That historical event took place on August 15, 1931, and brought new blessings and joy to her proud parents. The following Sunday I preached for Pastor Hyatt again — he was the pastor of the Luseland parish, which, by the way, was settled by a group of settlers from Nebraska, U.S.A. The place at which I preached was one of his preaching stations, Artland, which in 1936 signed the call that took me to my last place in Canada, to Lloydminster, where I began a congregation from scratch. More on that later.

Following my preaching engagement at Artland, we moved that week to Rosetown where a house had been rented from a doctor — Dr. Meyer — who became our family doctor. And a good one he was.

* * * * * *

The three of us arrived in Rosetown, Saskatchewan, on September 2nd. The few pieces of furniture we had — mostly second hand — were loaded on a truck of one of the Rock Haven members who delivered it.

September 3rd, company from Nebraska arrived — my wife's brother and a pal of his. Company at such a time! But we enjoyed them. What our visitors slept on has slipped my memory.

The day was far spent when we arrived in Rosetown. So was our energy. We needed light. So I connected the lead-in wires and there was light. I did not call the Power Company at that late hour. The next day they were at the house accusing me of stealing electricity and were ready to put me — a preacher — in jail. But being a preacher, I managed to talk myself out of that one. They listened to my persuasive words, installed a meter, and all was in good and harmonious order.

On Saturday, the Rev. Reitz arrived. His fourth visit in a year's time. Does that "make me out" to be quite a character who needed to be checked on frequently? No, he was not "checking" on me, but came to install me the first Sunday we were in Rosetown. Where? We had no church building in Rosetown. Only two or three Lutheran families, two of which lived out in the country. The family in town was only half Lutheran, or even less than half. The three families were: a garage man, a farmer, and a dairy man. We rented the Canadian Legion Hall right next to our member's garage and filling station. Before it could be used for an installation service, or any church service, it had to be cleaned.

The next day, Sunday, — I don't remember how the people were notified; I did not know any of them — we had the installation service. Rev. Reitz preached, installed me, and then I proudly performed a very distinct function, namely applying the Holy Sacrament of Baptism to our first-born daughter, by and through which she became a child of God and still is His child, serving him as a parochial school teacher in Faribault, Minnesota, where she found a shoe-maker's son, found it to be a good fit, stepped into a happy marriage with him, and it is wearing well, no repairs ever needed.

Having that company from Nebraska solved the problem of finding sponsors for our No. 1 daughter. That same week our company left again for home in Nebraska.

Rosetown parish was a newly created parish with two older preaching stations — Zealandia, 11 miles northeast, and Swanson, 55 miles northeast, which had been part of another parish. The Mission Board was realigning parishes mostly due to the depression which was still very severe with its dust storms. Will have more to say on the depression later.

Before long I added another preaching station which I opened west of Rosetown: Plenty. As time marched on, doing a lot of scouting and finding several Lutheran families in this and that area, I, in about one to one and a half years, had a parish of eight preaching stations, all (but Plenty) northeast of Rosetown and as far out as 60 miles. As much as possible, I served two or three preaching stations every Sunday and in the winter time I would serve them during the week so that I could tell to sinners the story of Jesus' love, and direct them to Him in Whom alone there is free, sure, complete, eternal salvation. At most places I also had Sunday School. At several places I had Sunday School teachers who would conduct Sunday School every Sunday. I tried to serve each preaching station at least once a month but did not always succeed, especially not in winter. During the winter I had to rely on the train, have some member meet me, take me to his home for a meal and a sleeping place, and take me to the place where the services would be held, mostly in homes of members in the winter. In between services I would have Sunday School and/or confirmation instruction.

For confirmation instruction I often made extra trips, especially in summer. Palm Sunday was not a "have to" for confirmation but whenever the children were ready. Adults I usually instructed during the week. Most of them, also the men, were quite satisfied that way, especially if the instructions could be given in the evening. One or two instances I shall never forget. One was where I had five adults, one man and four women if I remember correctly. I spoke to them about a public examination and confirmation at the very outset of the instruction. I asked them whether they would be willing to do it that way. "Oh, no!" one exclaimed. "I would be so nervous and scared that I could not answer any questions." I believe she was speaking for all of them. So I said, "Let's forget about that now and talk about it again when we have completed the instructions in God's Word." When that time had come, I put the same question to them again, public or private confirmation. The same lady quickly answered: "Public, of course, I now know the answers and am not ashamed to let people hear me confess the truth." They all felt that way. We rented a hall for the occasion. A large number of people came out for the confirmation which was held on a Sunday afternoon. We otherwise always held our worship services in the home of one member who had a home with ample room to hold the people who attended. This was at Swanson, about 50 miles east of Rosetown.

I had another preaching station at the next town north, Donnavon, where the services were conducted in the country, either in a school house or a home in the country. Service in a school was not possible when school was being held. Evening services in the school house in winter were not practical either because of the poor lighting. Remember, this is in the 30's, dirty 30's. As at Swanson, services here were also usually held in the same home, and as at Swanson, so also the people of this home met me at the train in winter time, kept me overnight, fed me, and took me back to catch the train again.

The home of the people at Donnavon was a small house, four rooms if I remember correctly. A person had to make sure not to walk too erect when walking through the doorway. But we packed 40 people into that home, mostly adults, who came to hear God's saving gospel of salvation in Christ and to worship Him with their hearing, singing, praising, praying, and offerings.

How did we do it?! The legs of their round dining table were taken off, the top rolled outside and leaned against the house. The legs were stacked up beside the table top. The buffet was shoved into the corner. Wood blocks, 10-gallon cream or milk cans were brought in, chairs with backs broken off and those still having backs were used, table boards and other boards or planks were laid onto the blocks, cans, chairs to make benches, then covered with blankets, quilts, robes for comfort and to protect from slivers. Also the beds in the bedrooms and the chesterfield (couch to us Americans) were used for seating. Pretty well in the middle of the house was my place where I stood and used an old sewing machine for an altar, a pulpit and lectern. I had people seated all around me except to my left where there was a wall. I believe this is where the idea of a round church came from. As a rule I served here in the evening because I had services in Swanson in the afternoon. Morning services I held, as a rule, in Rosetown where we lived. In my "spare time" I did some canvassing, made mission calls, sick calls, pastoral calls, and prepared and studied sermons. During the winter, of course, I had to use the train, not always a comfortable passenger train, but mixed trains, which means: a passenger coach was hooked on to the end of a freight train. It was heated by a pot-belly stove which I often kept going for the comfort of myself and other passengers, if there were any. Seldom were.

My car I usually set up on blocks for the winter — these are the 30's, don't forget, Readers — because roads were not kept open for auto travel. Travel was by means of horses and sleighs, sleighs of various description. Will give you one later on. I do it that way to keep you reading what I wrote "as I remember it."

Must tell you several unforgettable experiences that occurred at the Donnavon preaching station. I usually stayed overnight here, also in summer, so I could instruct a class of about 15 children in the chief articles of Christian doctrine with the hope that all would be confirmed and become members of the church. On one such occasion, the lady of the house — the same house in which we held our services — prepared a delicious supper for the whole class because, if I remember correctly, one of the class members had a birthday. After the supper the children went out to play. It was early fall. Our good hostess had raised a few turkeys, some of which were perched on the barn roof. It was getting dark and we had a gasoline lamp burning which hung by a window. Somehow or another the children must have frightened the turkeys and bang, crash, clatter, one of them flew in through the window. The lady of the house and I were still sitting at the table chatting. What a scare! But we managed to grab the turkey at once, and the lamp, which, of course, was not lit any more. Did any of you ever have a turkey so anxious to be on your table that it came flying through a window and landed on the table!?

Another unforgettable happening in this same home was: when after the conclusion of a worship service, I was packing my books and clerical robe into by club bag and I stood up straight again. As I did I bumped my head on the gasoline lamp which was hanging next to and over the "sewing machine" altar and pulpit. It came tumbling down, but I caught it before it landed on anything. I believe I saw stars but to comfort me a lady said, "Oh, that poor lamp!"

Another unforgettable experience was an unusual funeral. A somewhat mentally retarded girl gave birth to — as I was told — a still-born child. Some animal-like man probably had taken advantage of her. Over a period of weeks before the birth, I spent hours in her home, instructing her in the chief parts of Christian doctrine. I noticed several times that she was rather nervous and uncomfortable at times but had not the faintest idea that she was pregnant. She was naturally plump. I thought it as because of her mental problems. Hence, I was very patient and lenient with her. She did, however, study and learned the way to salvation. I confirmed her and communed her. The still-born child arrived a month or more after her confirmation.

The news of this birth came to me a month or longer after the birth. The lady and her husband told me about it after a worship service I held in their home at Donnavon. They had been asked to inform me and to ask that I bury the child. Believe me. I was shocked! I intended to go home again the day after the service. My dear wife was expecting me. There was no phone that I could call her. I stayed. The next day we went by sleigh to the home of the girl, about 8 miles, maybe more, I don't remember. It seemed much more because it was cold, brrr! After arriving at the girl's home, we had a brief service because we had at least 15 miles to the cemetery. We had to retrace our "steps." We stopped at the home where we had the worship service the evening before to warm ourselves a little. Before we could go to the cemetery we had to stop at the municipal office to inquire about a grave. No arrangements had been made for the burial.

The man responsible for a burial place had to go with us to show us where to bury the child. He scratched and dug in the snow for at least a half hour but did not find a stake. I was getting colder and colder. I believe the man from the municipal office was likewise, because he said, "Dig a grave here. If it is not in line, we will move it next summer."

Oh boy, I grabbed a pickaxe right quick and began swinging it, not only to get a grave dug but also to get my blood melted and circulating again and feel a little warmer. A few of the other men had the same idea. So before long we had a shallow grave dug. Now to place the casket (a wooden apple box) into the grave. One looked at the other but no one made a move. Instead they wanted to take their head gear off to show their respect. I admired them for that but I said, "we had our service at the home. Let us place the box into the grave and get out of this cold." But nobody made a move to do it. So I did. I grabbed the two ends of the box, a hand underneath each end. While letting the box slide down, one side slid faster than the other. My hands were so cold I could hardly bend my fingers. Well, when the box was not going down level, (we had not dug the grave quite long enough for the box to go down with a hand on each end of it) several of the men finally took over. They got the box down — I don't know how — closed the grave, and we were on our way.

He finally arrived at the place where I was staying. I could hardly walk.

My feet were so cold. I at once asked the good lady of the house to get me a pan of cold water so I could put my feet into it. She did. Oooh! Oooh! did my feet hurt! But I survived and still have my same two feet. The next day I went home. The man of the house took me to the train. By the time I arrived home I was sick, really sick, but have no explanation for it. A couple of days and I was ready for another such ordeal. Don't you believe it!

I hope that anyone reading this will fully realize that our missionaries in foreign fields endure many an inconvenience and hardship for the sake of Christ and His saving Gospel and I trust that the readers will pray more often for them and give more liberally and cheerfully for the missions of our church.

The people who offered their house for a place of worship had a family of three boys and one girl. There always was a short time of visiting after our services. During this time, the youngest of the boys, possibly four or five years old, crawled under the buffet and fell asleep there.

After all the people had gone and it was high time that the children go to bed, the youngest was missing. We searched everywhere. No boy anywhere. One of the families who came regularly for worship were relatives of the family in whose home the services were held. The father of the boy hooked his horses to the sleigh and drove to their place to inquire whether the boy had probably crawled into the back end of their cutter and fallen asleep there. The weather was quite comfortable. No boy there.

In the meantime, we moved the buffet and there under it was the boy. He had crawled under it and undoubtedly slept soundly. The father returned and all were happily united again, as I remember it.

At Rosetown progress in the church was very slow. I did a lot of canvassing, calling, etc., but the people were mostly churched. There were too many churches already for the size of the town. And in the country you did not find two or three families living on a section of land but rather one family living on two sections of land. Cross-roads going east and west were two miles apart. Going north and south there was — at least there was supposed to be — a road every mile. Farmers were wheat farmers and farmed six, ten, twelve, or more quarters. They did not measure the land by acres, but by quarters. Of course, about half the land was left idle for a year for a summer-fallow. This means that the country round about was rather sparsely settled.

Attendance at Rosetown did, however, increase a little. It averaged from 12 to 25. Two families lived about 5 and 12 miles south of Rosetown. One was a wheat farmer; the other a dairy man and wheat, oats, and sunflower farmer. The sunflowers he used for silage. These two families were the only members from the country and usually about half the attendance. The other people attending were residents of Rosetown. Our organist was a music teacher who was a Lutheran, but only by birth. I could not interest him in taking instruction to become a member. But he loved to play the piano and usually had his Sunday dinner with us. This was, I believe, the main thing that persuaded him to be our organist, or pianist, if you will, at our worship services.

Our place of worship in Rosetown was the Canadian Legion Hall, which we rented. Before we could conduct services there on Sunday morning, I had to get up extra early to get there to clean the hall of all the bottles, cigarette and cigar stubs, and all kinds of other rubbish left there from the Legion's parties of the night before. In winter I also had to get the fire going to warm the place and arrange the chairs for seating and the table or desk for an altar, lectern and pulpit. It also needed a little airing out before the service.

While living in Rosetown we had to buy our drinking water by the pail — 5¢ a pail. We had a galvanized barrel in the basement which the "Water Jack" filled, as a rule, twice a week. We learned how to save water. Oh, yes, Rosetown had a well, a very deep one, but the water was harder than iron and was hard on anything it was used for. So for washing clothes, we caught rain water in a tank and in winter when the tank was empty, we bought blocks of ice, which also were hard but the water was soft. Under such conditions, a person learns that good soft water, and any kind of water, is a blessing from God and one learns to appreciate good water.

At Zealandia, about 11 miles northeast of Rosetown, I had my largest preaching station in the parish. It was a country place where services were held in homes. It also was the oldest station. It had been served before I was stationed in the area but I don't remember from where. The majority of families I served lived along a creek which flowed through a beautiful, fertile valley. This majority totaled five families. As time marched on, I had a week-day Bible Class combined with a young people's organization which some of the older people also attended. I even had a choir for a short time. The farmers having cows that gave milk, which gave them cream, quite frequently made ice cream which was served not in cones or ice cream dishes but in soup bowls. Mmm, Mmm, good! I never saw anyone pack in as much ice cream as some of those young people did. Home-Made-Ice-Cream! (I hope I made your mouth water.)

In time some of the young people left home or got "hitched" and thus moved away, but not so far that they could not have come to church at least occasionally, especially in the summer time.

One of the families moved into the town of Zealandia. I then worked to hold services in town. I did several times but attendance was very small, not even our country people attending.

My place to stay while at Zealandia in the winter time was usually with a childless couple who really loved children. But the lady had more than enough cats which were in the house most of the time until 10:00 P.M. Then she would open the kitchen door, get the broom, pound the floor with it, and say "Skat! Skat! Skat!" and from all directions cats hurriedly made their way to the open door, except one. That was "Tommy," a spoiled and privileged cat or character. He lay sleeping under the heater — a wood and coal burning, round heater. (I write this explanation for the benefit of my modern readers.) Tom would never bother anyone and would not let anyone bother him. As a rule, when I got home, I had to clean the cat hair off my suit which I picked up from the Chesterfield. (Remember what that is? Not a cigarette.) The man of the house had his dogs, but only occasionally in the house, and as a rule, only one, a special German shepherd. The dogs were trained to take care of and drive his sheep which helped him through the depression which was still in full swing. The man of the house was not physically able to do the farming himself and he had much land. As a result, he had hired men almost all year. Money from the sheep paid their wages. Living in a valley next to a creek gave him pasture for the sheep.

At the home of these people I spent some of my most profitable, joyful, and interesting evenings which often lasted until two in the morning. They were faithful Bible readers. The man of the house learned to read only a short time before I began serving the Zealandia preaching station. He asked a nephew to bring him an English primer. He studied it and taught himself to read. Then he ordered an English Bible from me. This he read most diligently. It was slow and difficult at first, but he mastered it by being persistent. When he came upon something he just could not understand, he called his wife to come and read that part of the Bible to him in German. He, by the way, was not well and was in bed much of the time. If they could not get the meaning from reading it in the two languages, they would note the passage on a sheet of paper so they could ask me when I came. These discussions of the holy and saving word of God were truly some of the most happy and interesting and enlightening and faith-strengthening experiences of my ministry in Canada, as I remember it, even though the discussions lasted until two o'clock or a little later — or shall I say earlier — in the morning? And this lady also turned on a light in me with respect to some passages I had difficulty with. I shall gratefully remember these people as long as I live.

The man also told me the story of his younger life, when he was already a married man. I shall not reveal it but merely say that he lived a wicked life for some years. But God, who works in a mysterious way His wonders to perform, brought him back to the fold again and claimed him as one of His own. As long as there is life, there is hope. That man also gratefully acknowledged the saving grace of God.

There was a family in this preaching station — the sister of the man I just wrote about — who needed a special visit by the pastor, especially the young men in the family. So, one day in winter when I was there for worship and stayed the night as usual with the couple I wrote about above, I told the man of the house that I wanted to visit his sister's family — he knew why. He did not take me there but told me to use his team of horses and cutter and go there. This I did. They lived in the same valley along the creek about, oh, one, maybe two, miles west. It was a beautiful evening. I had my pastoral visit which lasted about two hours. I was ready to go back to my host's house. One of the older young men hooked my horses to the cutter and came in and reported that it was snowing and blowing some.

After bidding them "Good night" and thanking the young man for getting the horses and all ready, I left. I had to drive through a gate but in the dark and snow, which I had to face, I could not find the gate. I drove back and forth, finally got out of the cutter and walked back and forth leading the horses but still did not find the gate. What to do? I could barely see the light in the house. I went back. When I entered and told them that I could not find the gate, they laughed.

As soon as I had left, they prepared a lunch. They did ask me to have some before starting on the way home again. The horses were tied to a post.

One of the men lit a lantern to help find the gate. I was in the cutter following the light. He led us back and forth because he could not find the gate. After another try he found it, led the horses through the gate, then told me to let the horses go — they knew the way. I should try and watch the fence posts which were right alongside the trail. This I did and did see a post now and then, at least I thought I did. The wind and snow were more to my left and behind me. That told me that I was going in the direction I was supposed to go, namely east. Home was east. The wind therefore was from the northwest. But, oh, what happened now? The wind and snow is now blowing right into my face. The horses turned away from the fence.

I was cold and getting colder. But I was not frozen stiff — I was scared stiff. I tied the lines together, hung them over my shoulders, and prayed, yes, prayed that God would direct the horses and bring me home safely. I knew from my host that in a bad storm at night horses keep going in a circle to get the wind and snow out of their faces.

How true that is, I don't know, but I believed it and also believed this was the end for me. I could see no light, no nothin' anywhere. Now what? The wind and snow were not in my face anymore. Yep, the horses are going in circles. This is it!

Oh, what was that? It looked like a big gate post. It was! We had arrived safely at my host's place. The horses had more confidence than I did. And the reason for turning into the wind for a while was because the trail made a bend because the creek made a bend and came out under the fence. The fence was built straight through the creek. This was not told that evening, but learned it later in the daytime.

My host and hostess were quite concerned about me — yes, a little more than that, because when I came into the house, my host laid down the law to me and said: "The only good sense is to stay where you are in such weather." That can be understood in two ways: Stay in the house where you are or stay in the storm where you are. That they are concerned is proven by the fact that as soon as I was on the place, the good lady of the house came with a lantern and helped me get the horses unhooked from the cutter, get them into the barn, unharnessed, watered and fed for the night. This team, I learned later, was only three years old, a beautiful team of dapple-grey horses. Another proof that God answers prayer and delivers His people.

Another unforgettable experience at Zealandia was at the confirmation of a girl of the family I had visited the evening I was so frightened because of the snowstorm I was in. When a missionary-pastor has a far-flung parish of five or six preaching stations, confirmation day includes the examination in the chief parts of Christian doctrine, then a sermonette, then the rite of confirmation, followed by communion for the newly confirmed and the other members of the preaching station. Announcement or registration for communion would be done before the services.

This day two married sisters of the girl I confirmed that day also wanted to commune. They were not members and a few things I knew about them just would not let me permit them to commune at the Lord's Table. I did not accept their announcement and briefly told them why I could not accept them.

The father in this family, who was bedfast because he was so badly crippled from arthritis but was a devout, patient, cross-bearing Christian, told me when I visited him and communed him that the two girls had remarked that they were going to announce for communion just to see what the darn fool (meaning me) would say. He told me that he had begged them not to do such a thing and thanked me for refusing to commune them.

The Rosetown parish slowly grew larger by beginning new preaching stations, giving me more work but also more opportunities to declare the good news about Jesus, in whom alone there is salvation for sinners. My parish finally grew to ten preaching stations stretching 135 miles from east to west along the Canadian National Railroad, the main line from Saskatoon, Saskatchewan to Calgary, Alberta. The parish actually extended about ten miles into Alberta. There were three preaching stations there which had been vacated and by an arrangement between the Alberta-British Columbia District and the Manitoba-Saskatchewan District, these were added to my parish. To get there in winter, I boarded the train in Rosetown at 8:00 P.M. and arrived at my destination in the "wee" hours of the morning, long before day-light. But I had some fine, faithful Christian people there who received the Word with gladness as well as a few who caused a pastor some heartaches every now and then. That was a good reminder that I was still dealing with sinners and needed to apply the Law as well as the assurance of the saving Gospel of Christ.

There were three stations: one in Alsask, where we held services in the Anglican Church (Church of England, known here in the U.S. as the Episcopal Church); the second station was south of Alsask about ten miles where we held services in a school house or home; and the third at Sibbald, about eight miles west of Alsask. (Alsask, by the way, was right on the Alberta-Saskatchewan line, the fourth meridian.) Services at Sibbald were also held in a school house or home about six or eight miles north of Sibbald. This was the largest of the three preaching stations. The people were Germans, some of whom had escaped from Russia. Hence, here I conducted the services in German. If I remember correctly, I had only one other station on the very east end of my outstretched parish where I preached German occasionally, depending on who was present, or should I say absent. In those days I was able to preach a sermon in the German language, if I knew it and was able to preach it in the English language, without writing it in the German language. At most stations we had no pianist or organist. Neither was I one. So it was up to me to lead in the singing with my natural musical vocal chords. Very seldom I had any difficulty, except once which I still remember well. That was at Sibbald. My German music chords played tricks on me. I knew the melody of the hymn selected but in the third or fourth line there was a similarity to another melody and invariably I slipped into the wrong melody. Hence, we would not come out right on the next line and worse at the end of the stanza. So I stopped singing. The congregation likewise. I made a new beginning. The same problem. After three or four trials I asked if anyone knew the melody and would please lead us. A lady with a beautiful soprano voice knew the melody and began singing the hymn; the congregation followed her. I just listened. When she came to my trouble spot, she sang it without trouble. I joined in and everything came out correctly. It was a hymn with a goodly number of stanzas, I remember, and we sang enough of it to really learn the melody. That experience I call an embarrassing experience which a person would just as soon forget.

One other experience I had at Sibbald I will never forget took place on Easter Sunday. In my large, outstretched parish, I arranged festival services in such a way that each station would have a festival service on the day of the festival over a period of several years, at least the larger preaching stations. For example: those stations which had Christmas Day services would not have Easter Day services that same year or Pentecost Day services on the day of the festival.

I had scheduled Easter services for Sibbald, Alsask, and South Alsask. A day or two before Easter the weather became unusually warm. The snow was melting rather quickly. One of our members from Sibbald met me at the train and took me to his home in the country in a cutter. We had no trouble getting home because of the little snow and much mud. We had breakfast. Services were scheduled for the afternoon. His family and I were on our way. If I remember correctly, we were all in the cutter. The road was very muddy and the horses had a hard time pulling the cutter and staying on their feet in the slippery mud with frost underneath the mud. We decided to leave the road and go into the field where there were some piles of snow left here and there and we would go from one to the next. But the ditch was still full of snow and water underneath the snow. The horses broke through and their bellies were resting on the snow. They were very excited and lunged, fell down, but managed to get on their feet again. How fortunate that they didn't break the cutter tongue. The owner was out of the cutter in front of the horses and got them quieted down. Then he urged them on again and after a few desperate tries and lunges, they got us through the ditch into the field. Then we skipped from one snowbank — what was left of them — to another, heading for the home of another member who lived between us and the school house where the services were to be held. We made it.

From his place we had a good view of the school house. We had been watching whether anyone had come for the services. It was near the time that the services were to begin. No one had arrived. We watched for some time. Nobody there. I had a brief Easter service with the two families and then we made our way home again. Then back to Sibbald, using the fields as much as possible for navigation. I waited there for the train to go home again. It was impossible to get to either of the other two places and just as impossible for the people to get to the place of worship. That was an unforgettable Easter Festival and no Easter eggs either. I can still see those horses stuck in the snow in the ditch. I felt very sorry for them but even with a lot of "horse sense," they were not aware of my sorrow, I am sure.

But now to another all-important event. It happened on a bitterly cold night. My wife was in the Rosetown hospital. To keep her company, Vera

May, daughter No. 2, made her entrance into the world which made us happy.

All five of our girls were born in Canada but Vera May is the only one who chose Canada instead of the U.S.A. for her home country. A nice young man persuaded her to be and remain a good and loyal Canadian. Both are very faithful and diligent church workers. They have a truly Christian family of two girls and one boy.

Eleven days after Vera May came to live with us, I had the joy of baptizing her during a worship service in Rosetown and from that day on she also is a dear child of God and has her name written in the Book of Life.

Christmas was drawing near and Christmas programs were being rehearsed at the various preaching stations where we had enough children and a leader or teacher to be able to have a children's Christmas service. Some were presented before Christmas and some even after Christmas. In any case, the good news of glad tidings that the Savior, who is Christ, the Lord, was born, was told to sinners, all of whom need the Savior to have life eternal in heaven. He alone makes Christmas a "Merry Christmas."

In the Sibbald preaching station I had some people who escaped from the Communists in Russia. Stories they told of the persecution they had to endure are almost unbelievable. Christians were loaded into stockcars on the railroad and hauled into Siberia. There they were dumped out in the wilderness. There they suffered much. Many died, especially older people and babies. Some managed to escape and come to Canada. Among these was a mother who sat by a tree and just had to watch her baby die because she had no milk for the baby due to the lack of the right food. The people lived mostly on soup made from certain roots which they dug up and cooked. This mother had several other children and a husband, all of whom somehow managed to get out of Siberia and then came to Canada. They were a fine Christian family and grateful for their deliverance into freedom.

At Harris, Tessier, and Laura, 22 to 35 miles east of Rosetown, I had been doing some mission work and found some Lutherans who were more or less interested. The one man who was mostly responsible for the establishment of a preaching station in that area was a Lutheran. His first wife had died. Later he married a widow who had a son. The man could not read nor write. We held services in a country school if the service was held on Sunday and during the summer when the school house was not in use; otherwise, we held services in his home. I instructed his wife and her son and in time confirmed them. I also had Sunday School with the children that were present.

This unusual man would always listen carefully when I was instructing his wife and her son. Certain Bible verses that struck him, he had his wife say them to him until he had them memorized. Likewise with certain hymn stanzas. He asked me for some of the Sunday School leaflets with the beautiful colored pictures on them. Then he would hook his horses to his buggy and drive from place to place speaking to people about Jesus, doing real mission work, leaving some of the Sunday School leaflets in homes where there were children. He enjoyed doing this. In the course of several months he gathered an adult class of five for me to instruct in God's Word. This I did and in time confirmed them. They also bought Bibles and became diligent Bible readers. What joy these kinds of happenings bring into a missionary-pastor's life! Oh, the many happy, unforgettable hours I spent in the home and company of this illiterate but well-informed man — well-informed in the one thing needful for eternal salvation.

While serving the Rosetown parish, my Model T was becoming more and more decrepit from old age, just like the "old gray mare." So I traded for a 1924 Chevrolet sedan. Wow! was I coming up in the world! What a "classy" car for a missionary to drive during the depression which was still very serious. We still had, by far, more dust storms than rain storms or even snow storms. And some roads and trails were blocked by dust drifts. Often I would get stuck in a dust drift. It was almost impossible to shovel yourself out. I always carried a shovel with me. The dust would blow or fill in the trail just about as fast as one could shovel it out. Oh, how the rear wheels would jerk, quiver and quake in the dust drifts. Often I would turn into the fields (there was little or no crop except Russian thistles) and find my way through the field between the drifts of dust where the top-soil was blown away. There were few fences, mostly open range. Most crop-land, however, was fenced.

During these depression years, many wells went dry. Cattle became poorer. The government bought many of them for one cent a pound. Also, people from the north among the lakes and trees bought cattle off the dried out prairie and made a big profit in that business. Families on the prairies used the Russian thistles for feed. They had to be cut when still young but even then many horses died from them. There was very little tractor farming at that time. Most of the people, if not all of them, on the prairie were on government relief for food, fuel, feed, and seed. Food given was mostly navy beans and turnips. We also had some. The seed was supposed to be paid back but I doubt that much of it ever was. Another story about the depression will explain why I believe it was not paid back. That story comes later. (So, if you want to know it, you will just have to read on. Tricky, ain't I?)

The feed the people were promised did not always come in time and often was very poor feed, much of it slough hay and reeds from up north among the lakes. One farmer who had about 30 head of cattle came into town day after day for the feed but it did not arrive. After a week or ten days of this and his cattle lacking sufficient water and thus bellowing day and night, the farmer took his 30-30 rifle and shot every one of them. He just was not able to endure the bellowing any longer.

One more remark about the Sibbald preaching station. There was one Jewish farmer in the community who attended my services occasionally. Because of this one Jew, a good neighbor, the members called the preaching station "Jerusalem."

In the summer time I usually served three stations on Sundays, never less than two. That meant two or three sermons each week, Sunday School, confirmation class, calls — in addition to driving from 60 to 100 miles that same day, one way. Attendance would average from eight or ten to 25 or 30 at the various stations. In the winter I would get around by train, but not always passenger trains. (Several pages back I wrote that I traveled in winter by train, often mixed trains, which I have already described.) Using a mixed train would give me a chance to catch up on sleep while the train was shunting freight cars around. The coach during that time was parked. But a person would find out with a sudden jolt when the coach was recoupled to the freight train. A member of the respective preaching station would meet me and take me to his house for a meal and then to the place of worship if the service was not being conducted in his home.

At one point the mixed train had to cross a river and then had a fairly steep incline to make to get to the next town on the top and level ground where I got off. Every now and then the freight train was too long to pull the whole train up the hill to the next town. So they left part of the train, including the coach, down at the river, pulled part of the train into the next town, then came back with the engine to get the remainder of the train. On those occasions I really did catch up on sleep. It was only occasionally that there were more passengers than I. The usual speed going up the hill was a "walking speed."

One time I remember the train crew must have been of the opinion that they could make the incline with the whole train. My, oh, my, did the engine puff and huff and puff and spin its wheels. Our speed was about that of an aged snail. Finally we were not moving ahead but going backward, picking up speed until the conductor pulled the emergency brakes and stopped the train. He walked to the engine. The fireman was a new and young man and did not know how to keep the steam up to the limit. The conductor ordered him to do a better job of firing. After some time the steam "popped off." The train was backed slowly down the hill while the fireman was shoveling coal. Back down on the level ground, the engineer started for the incline again, picking up speed as he approached the hill; but it was a "walking speed" again before we reached the top.

There was an attempt made to keep at least the main roads open until Christmas. After that I set my car up on blocks and depended on trains and sleighs to haul me from place to place and to keep warm I often walked (and at times ran) behind the sleigh, unless I was fortunate enough to have the pleasure of riding in a closed-in sleigh with a small stove in it. There were few such conveniences and luxuries in the 30's and early 40's, not even toilets in the homes with exceptions in the larger towns and cities — and many of these were not "flush stools." There were very few sewer systems. Once a week the "honey wagon" would come after midnight and empty the "indoor luxury." A rain-pipe directed into the chimney took out the "aroma." Air fresheners were also unknown in those "good old days."

Using trains and sleighs, I would conduct services during the week at most places, possibly two to four stations which would mean that in a month's time I would possibly be away from my wife and family more days than would be with them. But God gave me a very good, patient, and enduring wife and helpmeet who also was an excellent mother and gave our girls a truly good and Christian foundation to build their lives on. Each one did and is now serving the Lord in the church in some phase of church work and is also bringing up our grandchildren in the fear and admonition of the Lord. This gives Christian grandparents much peace and joy! As I wrote above, in the winter time I served my parish by train and sleigh during the week and, as a rule, was home on Sunday to conduct services in the town in which we lived.

Once a month, sometimes twice a month in winter, I went on a coyote hunt. This takes us back to the illiterate man but a consecrated Christian and missionary who memorized Bible verses and hymns by having his wife repeat them to him until he knew them. (I wrote about him several pages back.) This man, as a rule, met me at the train, which was early in the forenoon. Services were scheduled for the afternoon. In winter he hunted coyotes to get a little money. This was during the depression when there were very little or no wheat crops — more "no" than "little." He lived near a lake which was almost dry now. There were some bluffs of scrubby trees. On our way home from the train we hunted coyotes with dogs which he had in a doghouse on his sleigh. He carried no gun with him. He knew the ways of the coyotes, could track them, and often ran one out of the bluff into the open field or prairie — then the chase began. He opened the door of the doghouse, out the dogs jumped — one catcher and one killer, and then his ponies would gallop like mad after the dogs and we — at least I — would hang on for dear life. That was some ride over "stick and stone." But, oh, it was exciting and fun! In the afternoon the worship service was conducted in his house. In the evening we discussed Bible passages. The next day, instead of taking me to the train, he took me "cross country" to the next preaching station. We left in good time so we could hunt coyotes on the way. This was a good variety of life in the life of a missionary on the prairie of Saskatchewan, and a good tonic. Did we catch any coyotes? What a question! Of course we did, but not every time. It still was fun and good variety of life for any missionary in Canada, the land of opportunity and promise.

The member at Zealandia who had taught himself to read and with whom I discussed Scripture into the wee hours of the morning had a five-strand barbed wire fence to keep his sheep in. This fence really caught and held the Russian thistles and the dust. Before long his fence was completely buried in a huge bank of dust. With the thistles in it, it became so firm that in time a person could drive over it. That was where the top soil of his own field was piled up.

As the depression years continued, the banks, loan companies, and machine companies repossessed what the people had bought but could not pay for. People who had bought land signed quit-claim-deeds because the interest they now owed was more than the principal. They packed what they still had on wagons, hay or bundle racks, hooked their skinny horses to them, tied their cows to the racks or had someone ride a horse to keep them moving, and headed north toward the lakes and bush country. This is a reason, I believe, the "relief seed" was never repaid.

My illiterate but sincere Christian and busy missionary had to give up his farm — likewise, most of the people he won for Christ and the Church whom I had instructed and confirmed. So that station died.

But I must tell you of one of those converts. When we studied baptism, I asked each of the five whether they were baptized and whether they were positively sure. All were sure but one. He said, "I must be because my mother did make me go to Sunday School regularly. Surely she had me baptized. But I will write to her and ask her." She lived somewhere in Alberta. There still was time enough to get an answer from her. But no answer came. He finally said, "Yes, I am sure that I was baptized." I had to take his word for it. But to be baptized again would have been better than to live in doubt. But he was sure. The confirmation of the class took place. They also received the Lord's Supper. It was a happy unforgettable event and an important one. My illiterate member beamed with joy

Several months had gone by. Here comes this man who was sure he was baptized with a letter from his mother. He was very excited. I tried to calm him and took him into my office. There he told me that his mother wrote that he was NOT baptized. "Oh, what will I do now? What will happen to me? Here I have had the Lord's Supper and am not even baptized yet," he said rather excitedly. I told him in a quiet and cool manner that no harm had been done. "We will baptize you and all will be in order. You did not deliberately lie or despise and reject baptism," I assured him. A week or so later, he was baptized in his home and our good missionary, who was responsible for bringing him into the church, was also present and again beamed with joy.

An unforgettable experience took place when I took the train to Deslisle, a preaching station at the east end of my "elongated" mission parish. When I stepped off the train that morning, there was no one there to meet me. Somehow there was a mix-up in dates or something. I don't remember any more. I just stayed in the depot, hoping. But several hours went by. Nobody showed up except some strangers. Services were to be in the afternoon. I finally asked a stranger whether he knew so and so and whether he had seen him in town. The first answer was "Yes"; the second, "No." After some time I asked another stranger and he said that he had seen him in town but he had gone home. Phone him? Few people had such a luxury. Another stranger came in who recognized me. He asked where I was going. I told him and he offered to take me there. He was a neighbor to my host.

This man was a very religious man. Before long we were in a long conversation on religion. He knew what I was. He belonged to a Holiness Body like the Pentecostals or Four Square Gospel. He did not believe in infant baptism but knew that I did. I was very much on my guard in what I answered him. I did not say exactly what he had hoped I would say. I was aware of that. I did bear witness to the truth, however.

Our conversation seemed to have ended. But only for a short time. He then asked me point blank with the hope of getting the answer he wanted from me: "So you believe that since you were baptized as an infant you are saved?" I confessed my faith in God's promise: "Baptism does also now save us." Then for about five miles we discussed, or should I say argued, infant baptism. In the course of the discussion he told me exactly when and where he was saved. It was while he was plowing. All of a sudden he received the Spirit and was saved; and from that time on he was a saved and different man. If and as long as he firmly believes in Jesus, the Son of God, and trusts in Him as the only Savior, he, too, will be in heaven with all the true believers in spite of his misunderstanding. It is unbelief, denial and willful rejection of the saving Gospel that damns. "Believe in the Lord Jesus Christ and you shall be saved," says God in His Word, the Bible. If any one does not know Jesus Christ or knows Him but does not believe in Him, such a person cannot and will not be saved.

Well, my "chauffeur" delivered me to the place I wanted to go. There was a mix-up in dates for services but we managed to notify a few and I conducted a worship service in the German language for them. That same evening I managed to catch my train for home again. Such trips are hard on the Mission treasury because collections were small just like the people's income during the depression. Offerings in church ranged anywhere from eighty cents to three or four dollars. Salaries people pledged seldom were paid in full by the end of the year. But our merciful and loving Lord and God never failed us but always filled the needs. The next story is one of my experiences which proves that fact.

It was summer, shortly before we moved to Harris. One of my members in Rosetown, as I already wrote, had a garage and filling station. I stopped there for gas but had no money and asked whether he would charge it. He would not. There was no credit in those hard times. I had a trip to make to several preaching stations about 60 miles one way. Uh, oh. While at the station the left rear tire goes flat.

My wife was with me. We must have asked the neighbor lady, a widow and a wonderful person, to care for our two girls while their mother was with me uptown.

I repaired the tire myself. While I was doing that, my wife walks to the post office. There could be no mail for us because we got our mail in the evening and this was afternoon. But she brought a letter from the man at Zealandia who usually kept me up till the wee hours in the morning discussing Scripture. There was a short branch line which made one round trip per week. The letter came on it. It contained a ten dollar bill. Wow! How mysteriously but wonderfully the Lord works.

If I remember correctly, that was the only letter I ever got coming in on that mixed train. My tire was repaired, my gas tank was full, and I still had some money left to take with me on the trip. Oh, yes, I would have gone anyway. I trusted that the offering would be enough to buy gas to get me home again. Canada uses the imperial gallon which is nearly a quart more than our U.S. gallon. And gas was much cheaper in those days than it is now. Our wonder-working God and Father in Christ knew what I planned to do to serve Him and my parish so He graciously filled the need and put us at ease. "How great Thou art!" Oh, if all of us would only realize and remember that more often and be truly grateful.

While we were still living in Rosetown, I became very sick with erysipelas.* It was a Saturday afternoon that we went to the doctor's office to see him about my wife's ingrown toe nails, or was it a goiter† which was troubling her. She had both. While we were there he noticed a small spot on my left cheek right under my left eye. "Oh," I said, "that

*A form of cellulitis, a potentially serious bacterial infection affecting the skin. It is also known as St Anthony's fire due to the intense rash associated with it.

†Abnormal enlargement of the thyroid gland. It is a butterfly-shaped gland located at the base of the neck, just below the Adam's apple. A large goiter can cause a cough and make it difficult to swallow or breathe.

is just a pimple." "No," he said, "that is erysipelas and very contagious and spreads very fast and is hard on the heart. You should be in the hospital in isolation with a special nurse. But if you do exactly what I tell you, you can be at home in a separate bedroom and nobody is to enter that bedroom except your wife and so I will save you some money. I will come to see you every day, maybe twice a day until we have it under control." But I refused and argued that tomorrow I have worship services to conduct. "No," he said, "you will not conduct services tomorrow. We will notify them that you are sick." He then gave my wife instructions and gave her a few small tablets of poison which she was to dissolve in a quart of water — not to give me to drink but to soak a cloth in and lay on my face a certain number of times during the twenty four hours of each day. He warned her to be most careful because she had enough poison there to kill all the dogs in town.

Before leaving the office, he applied pure carbolic acid around both my eyes to prevent it from spreading into my eyes. On our way home I informed the owner of the garage that there would be no services and asked him to try to let others know. I then went to bed. The next day my face was really swollen because the erysipelas had spread so fast. I was glad to be in bed and was thankful I had such a good "nurse" to take care of me. In time the Good Lord restored me to health so that I could serve my parish again and tell people the story of Jesus and His unlimited love for sinners, every sinner.

The best preaching stations and the most of my members were 20 to 60 miles east of Rosetown. The soil at Rosetown was good for wheat but not for garden. There was a nice place with a good house and some other buildings and a big garden about a quarter mile east of Harris for rent, and for less rent than we paid in Rosetown. So we moved. It was a good place for our two girls to grow up and I was closer to most of my preaching stations and I was still on the same railway line. Rosetown itself gave no hope of a congregation. There is no Lutheran church there to this day.

Finances were still very tight because of the depression. Salaries did not go up except the seniority system of the District would add one dollar a month up to ten years. The idea of the system was to keep the missionaries from America in Canada. Western Canada — especially in the prairie provinces — was still virgin mission fields.

We liked the place. It had a well so now we did not have to buy water at 5¢ a pail anymore. There were some trees and a garden that was workable and produced, but we had to do some watering. The depression and dust storms were still with us. But the garden helped our grocery bill. We even canned some vegetables.

Telephone and fence posts were very smooth and shiny on the west side, being polished by the dust. The wind was almost always from a westerly direction.

* * * * * *

Missionaries were permitted a two-week vacation per year but were allowed to let them pile up to six weeks, never more. This is what we did. So, our third year in Canada was our first trip back to the States to show off our two lovely girls to the grandparents and aunts and uncles and cousins.

Somewhere I got ahold of a small hammock which could be hung from the roof inside the car. The car roofs in those days still had some wood in them. I inserted two hooks and there we hung the hammock for one of the girls. The other girl slept on the back seat. Mama and papa slept in the front seat, if I remember correctly. We could not afford a motel or hotel. I can't even remember how we got enough money to make that trip of 1300 miles one way. Must have saved some and added it to the check we received from the Mission Board just before we left on our adventure.

I had the 1924 Chevy sedan checked out before leaving. The trip home was quite uneventful except for my wife taking the wrong highway in the wrong direction while I was sleeping. That part of the road was terrible, full of holes and ruts and no gravel. I was of the opinion that we were going in the opposite direction because I felt that we should have reached the town at which we planned to stop for the night quite some time before this. It was near midnight. We stopped so we might get our bearings by the North Star. But it was too cloudy to find it. We moved on but not far because the car stalled. I tried to find the trouble, but did not. So we decided to sleep till it was daylight.

Yes, I could sleep. A missionary in western Canada in those days was always tired and could sleep anywhere — almost — even on a straw mattress with one or two slats missing. I could also sleep with bedbugs but my wife definitely could not. Will tell you about that a little later.

We were sleeping in the stalled car. Before long a big car came with several men in it. They stopped and asked whether they were on the right road to Moose Jaw. I said, "Yes, can't be very far ahead." That is where we wanted to stay that night. They offered us no help which I did not regret because I think they were "loaded." Their speech betrayed them. But they were going in the wrong direction, just as we were, which I discovered when the sun made its appearance in the "west." "This is odd," I said, "for centuries, many centuries — at least, up to this day — the sun had come up in the east." We were headed in the wrong direction.

I then looked for the reason our car had stalled. It was not because we were going in the wrong direction and were almost as far north as we were when we left home, only farther east. No, the reason was: the cable on the battery broke. (That could not happen on a Model T. They had coils instead of a battery. The Moral: Drive a Model T.) I somehow wired it together again. We then faced our Chevy sedan in the opposite direction and were on our way. In Moose Jaw, if I remember correctly. I had a new cable installed. From there on we sailed along smoothly. Our two girls don't remember anything of that night on the road heading in the wrong direction. It was just another night for sleep to them. Oh, the blessing of being a small child and having no problems, troubles and worries — at least no worries.

We crossed the border at North Portal and had no difficulties with the customs officers. We arrived at Grandma's house safely. But they paid little attention to the proud parents of the two "darling" girls. Well, that's the "way" of grandparents. But we did get attention later on and royal treatment and were loaded down with all kinds of canned food when we left again three weeks later.

Our trip back home to Canada was not so good. Shortly before we crossed the line into North Dakota, our Chevy was heating and boiled the water away. We stopped at a filling station and before I could say enough, a lady attendant poured cold water into the radiator and cracked the block of the motor, which I discovered some miles later when the radiator was steaming again. I stopped at a filling station to let the motor cool off. There an attendant looked for the reason and found a small crack in the block of the motor. He sent me to a garage. He said the best thing would be to get a new block. When he told me how long it would take and what it would cost, I said, "I do not have that much money." He said, "well, I could try to seal it and get you by for a time, but I cannot guarantee that it will hold." I do not remember what it would cost, but I told him to repair it.

We had to stay the night there. But where? I asked about a Lutheran church. There was one, Missouri Synod. I went to the pastor and told him my "hard luck" story. He and his wife most graciously took us in for the night. The next day we were on our way. We arrived home safely in Canada. Again, no problems with the customs officers.

Second-hand cars kept me badly broke. I could not afford a new car, but neither could I afford a second-hand car — buying and paying for someone else's troubles. I had a Model T, a Chevy, a Plymouth, a Hudson, a Model A, an Oldsmobile, and a few more — almost too numerous to mention. Everything but a Maxwell. Two of the best of the whole lot were the Model T and the Model A. (If the president of Ford Motor Company were to read this, possibly he would present me with a Lincoln as a token of appreciation for saying this about my two "Fords.")

Just before the "vacation" story, I wrote about the telephone and fence posts being polished on the west side. That is a few pages back. The wind did not stop blowing and the depression did not go away while we were gone and there were still Russian thistles around. I wrote that because the depression verily brought hard times and people were moving north where the lakes and bush were. It was quite often that one would see a caravan of five to ten wagons and racks and cattle on the road heading north. That is what my largest preaching station did. I served them twice a month. One week on Sunday I was there to conduct services, had a good attendance, a lady teaching Sunday School every Sunday, a class of twelve or fifteen confirmands; 90% of them from unchurched or non-Lutheran homes, and I had the hope that all would become members of the church. Two weeks later when I was there again for services, there were none of them there anymore except one family with one son. Will tell you more about this family later.

The others had packed the little they had in racks and wagons and headed north. This one family I want to write about later also started north with the others but turned back. I do not remember now why they turned back. My parish was "drying up" just like everything else. Even a goodly number of the few trees that were there died. The country was not a pleasant sight to behold.

Why does God send such adverse things upon a land and its people and beasts? To remind us of sins and our sinfulness and that we need Him and cannot carry on without His blessings and that we owe it to Him to live grateful lives. We forget so often to say: "Thank you, God!"

Also, some of my other preaching stations were shrinking. The Board of Missions then had ideas of moving me further north again and dividing my Rosetown parish, adding some stations to this parish and some to that parish, and thus giving these neighboring parishes more members. But before we move, I have some stories or experiences to tell yet, as I remember them.

The lady that taught Sunday School every Sunday in the preaching station that moved north was instrumental in bringing the family with the one son — the family I referred to before and promised to tell more about — to Christ and into the church.

The man of this family was a distant relative of the Sunday School teacher. He came from a Lutheran family but had been unchurched for some years. He told me about some of his unchurched and unchristian life. His wife was of the United Church of Canada. She was a divorcee and had a son when he met her. Sometime after they were married they moved into the area where the Sunday School teacher lived. This was before I had a preaching station there. The family of the Sunday School teacher, who had four children, occasionally attended an Anglican church service. When I began a preaching station in the area, they faithfully attended and worked for it.

They brought the family with the one son to church. This family had an addition to the family. But the child was very sick and not expected to live. The lady Sunday School teacher insisted that the child be baptized, which the parents seemingly were not concerned about. I was told about it by the Sunday School teacher and, if I remember correctly, I baptized the child in the hospital with the consent of the parents. The child died soon after that. As time moved on, the parents and son attended my services occasionally. Both the Sunday School teacher and I were working on them.

Another baby arrived who, likewise, was a sick baby, but lived longer. I baptized the child. He was in and out of the hospital for some time. He also passed away. The parents were more receptive now to God's Word and attended church more regularly. The lady dearly loved little children and both of her children being taken from her gave me an opportunity to get close to her with the saving Gospel. In the course of time, I instructed her in the Christian doctrine. During this time she became sick and was in bed for some time. I made extra trips — about 60 miles one way — to instruct her and then make other calls. While she was sick in bed, I told her that I would come back some other time when she felt better. "Oh, no, you don't," she said, "you sit right down next to my bed and teach me. This is the most important thing for me now." She was a good student, studied and memorized much. In due time I confirmed her and no pastor could wish for more faithful members and Bible students. A number of times she told me how thankful she was that her children were baptized. This was a real comfort to her and gave her and her husband real joy. They never were rich in the things of this world, but were a most content and happy family rejoicing in the spiritual, eternal riches they now possessed.

Well, a year or two after that preaching station (where this family had membership) had moved north, they also moved north, but not as far. They moved into the Battleford area. The Board of Missions had already moved me and my family to Lloydminster, which was on the fourth meridian — the Alberta-Saskatchewan boundary line. We made this move in the fall of 1936.

* * * * * *

Before moving, we made a trip to Lloydminster to find a house to live in. The town had a population of about 1,200. It was — and still is — about 300 miles north of the U.S. border. Houses were very scarce. The town had two railway lines: the Canadian National and the Canadian Pacific. It was a terminal point for the C.P. The C.P. was drilling a well for water but struck a gas vein. That brought in various oil companies who were drilling here and there to find more gas, but they also struck oil. Now the rush was on! That is why houses were scarce. We did find a small house, hardly large enough for all our second-hand furniture — we could not afford to buy new — and our family of four. Our third child was on the way and so we would be a family of five — could have been six; who knew — in a four-room house, and they were small rooms, too. But we had no choice. We rented it and then drove back to Harris and prepared to move. I don't remember how we moved.

Trying to remember how we moved. I suddenly became aware of the fact that I have three other experiences I wanted to write about before telling you about moving to Lloydminster. I shall tell them now and then pick up the "moving thread" again.

I must take you back in time one year, to the winter of 1935-36. Some time before Christmas 1935, the District Board of Missions instructed me that right after New Year I should go up north and try to "round up" the children I had in confirmation class in the preaching station that moved north, complete the instruction and confirm them. I had reported to the Mission Board what had happened to this preaching station right after the people had moved north.

I did make the trip up into the bush and it is one of the most unforgettable trips I made. My wife and our two daughters had gone to the States to Grandma's house quite some time before Christmas. It was what the doctor ordered because of my dear wife's health. She had an inward goiter which was sapping her strength and health away. He put her on medication and sent her back to mama to regain some strength before she could have the goiter removed by operation. One thing he wanted her to drink was a bottle of beer every day. But she hated beer. So I drank most of the beer and that seemed to help her. I was happy to help her.

So I was home alone. What a lonely feeling to come home to an empty and cold house from my mission trips!

I informed my parish — what was left of it — what the Board of Missions instructed me to do. Right after New Year I set my car on blocks — I don't remember what make of car I had then — and prepared to head north into the bush. Several days before Christmas the temperature started going down, down, down. Brrr, it was cold! We had had a goodly amount of snow, too. I locked the house and made my way to the depot to catch the morning train. In Saskatoon, the city beautiful, I had to change trains, but that would be the next morning. I stayed the night with the pastor and his family. I had written the lady who taught Sunday School every Sunday while living on the prairie that I was coming and for what purpose. Her son was one of the confirmands. The second train I had to take left the next morning. To get to the depot I took the street car because I did not expect the pastor and family to get up that early, give me breakfast, and take me to the depot on a cold, cold morning. Some of you reading this possibly do not know what a street car is and looks like. Ask your Grandpa and Grandma.

When the street car was about three-fourths of the way to the depot, we were delayed by a one-horse sleigh loaded with coal that was stuck on the street car track. The cold steel runners on the sleigh just would not slide over the cold steel rails. He turned his horse back and forth, whipped it, jiggled the sleigh, worked hard to get off the track. I felt sorry for both man and beast but was more worried about catching my train. After about ten or thirteen minutes of jiggling, pushing, etc., he did get off the track and we were on our way again, with my grips in hand I stood at the door, ready to jump out as soon as the street car stopped. The stop was one block from the depot. As soon as the door opened at that stop, I was out and running to the depot. Oh, it was cold! As soon as I was in the depot I asked the station master about my train. It was just pulling out. He tried to catch and stop it, but failed. Now what do I do? That train would come back the next day and the day after that it would go my way again. There I was. Two days to do what?

To stay in a hotel and eat at the "chinks" — that is what we called most cafes because most of them were operated by the Chinese — was impossible. I could not afford it. The only thing left to do was go back to the pastor's house. This I did and, thank God, the pastor's family was so understanding and kind. Well, isn't that what people expect of a pastor's family?

One thing I had to do is let the family that was to meet me at the train know what happened, but I just don't remember how I did inform them.

Two days later — it was colder — I was on my way again to the bush. This time there were no delays on the street car. The train left on time and I was on it. Prince Albert was the end of the line for this train. There I would have to take a third train. Each one was a passenger train. Oh, yes, I was traveling first class!

Before arriving at Prince Albert, the train was three or four hours late. Some class! It was well past noon by the time we arrived at Prince Albert. There was no news boy on the train selling apples, peanuts, candy bars, cigarettes, etc., besides newspapers and magazines. Was I hungry! Just like a growing boy. The oatmeal I ate early that morning at the pastor's house, which his wife prepared the night before and kept warm in a double boiler on the stove, just did not stick to my ribs that long. The train should have been in Prince Albert by noon. I would have had ample time to eat a noon lunch.

The depot was at the edge of town and had no lunch counter nor was there a cafe anywhere near the depot and my next train was waiting or the train from Saskatoon. I asked the conductor about time to get a bit to eat. He said there would be no time. I then asked him whether the train I was to go on next would have a boy selling peanuts, candy bars, etc. Now I do not want to call him a liar, but he did not tell the truth because there was none. I could have eaten raw oysters by this time, and thinking of that I lose my appetite.

It was quite a while before train No. 3 left Prince Albert. I could have cooked a dinner before it finally left. It was late afternoon when I arrived at my destination; yes, it was beginning to get dark already. Would the couple who were to meet me be there? This question raced around in my head. I knew the first thing I was going to ask them about. It was at least five o'clock when I stepped off the train. "There they are," I said to myself, but to them I said, "is there a cafe here, and if so, take me there. I am starving." "Oh, no," said the lady. "There is a family just a mile from here who wants us to come there for a turkey dinner." Oh, what wonderful news; like sweetest music to my ears, or rather to my stomach. "Come on; let's do," I said, and then I greeted them.

We were off on a one-mile ride in a closed-in sleigh with a small heater in it to a turkey dinner — the longest mile ever for my stomach. When we arrived we were invited into the house. During introductions my eyes fell on the stove — they did not actually fall out on the stove, and if they had, they would not have been burned because the stove was cold and there were no kettles on it filled with food. I could not see a turkey in whatever direction I turned my eyes. We were ushered into another room. There was a cupboard, chairs, a table, but no food on it. We were asked to sit down. Good thing or I may have fallen over from weakness.

It was at least six in the evening. It was dark outside. We visited. It was seven. We visited some more. I had developed a headache by this time. To have something in my mouth I smoked cigarettes. By now it was eight o'clock. No food yet, but more visiting. The man and his wife who met me at the train and took me to this unusual "turkey dinner" in the home of this family, whose name I just do not remember — how could I, being so hungry for "turkey," looked at me again and again and I could see that they felt embarrassed and also sorry for me because on that long mile I told them about my stomach's desperate situation.

The evening moved slowly on. It was nine o'clock. Still no food, only visiting and smoking. Oh, look. The lady of the house gets up. She goes to the cupboard. My eyes follow her. She opens the cupboard door. A big loaf of bread appears at almost ten o'clock. She slices it. Butter and bread are put on the table. The "Gobbler" had not come out as yet to make his appearance. Neither had any "Mrs. Gobbler." As I remember it, I was watching and observing every move of the lady of the house and every door on her cupboard which she opened was bare of turkey. We had bread, butter, some kind of meat, I believe, (but not turkey) and some jelly and coffee. I ate almost a loaf of bread by myself. It was now after ten o'clock and we were now ready to go to the home of the people who met me at the train and took me to that delicious "turkey dinner." Never did get an explanation on that affair. Could that man stuck on the street-car track with his one-horse sleigh in Saskatoon be the culprit who beat me out of a turkey dinner and gave me that headache?

The horses were hooked up to the sleigh. The fire in the little heater was burning. It was a wood burning heater. We entered through the door in the back, closed it, and were on our way. I do not remember how many miles we had to go but it was a long way, for it was 2 A.M. before we were home. On the way we upset once in a big snow drift. We quickly crawled out through the door and set it up again and away we went. The thing we were traveling in was a house about twice the size of a 4-holer. (If some of you readers do not know what a "4-holer" is, ask Grandma or Grandpa.*) This was fastened on the front runners of a bobsled, had a window in the front end and a slit wide enough to get the lines through. The stove was fastened so it could not upset and a smoke stack went through the roof. The better or fancier ones also had a window in the back or the sides. It was very comfortable in there, so much so that one could take overcoat and mittens off. There were a goodly number of them by now, all shapes and sizes. In severe cold or deep snow, the horses could be given lots of time while the people remained comfortable.

The house these people lived in was a log house. It was old and had been used for a granary to store wheat. When they and their four children came from the prairies into the bush and lake country, the house was

*In 1955 the Buick Century and Super were given 4 VentiPorts per side on the front fenders behind the front wheels.

empty so they moved into it. In many places the mud between the logs had fallen out and one could see the outside without looking through the few windows there were in the house. There were two large rooms downstairs — a kitchen and a living room. They closed the kitchen because of the severely cold weather, 65° below zero for more than several mornings. They used only the one room in which they had an airtight heater. Bedrooms were upstairs.

The lady of the house did the little cooking she did on the airtight heater. Everything we wanted to eat had to be thawed out first. In the evening before the parents retired, we would have tea and a piece of bread or a cookie. That was about midnight. The man of the house kept the heater going good until that time. Then I took over till about 2 A.M. while reading the story book *The Wandering Jew.*

Everything was "dead still" except the stove. One night while reading a very spooky part of the story, there was a sudden thud against the house when a rabbit being chased by an owl ran against the house. That scared me so that I felt the chills running up and down my backbone. Or the shooting of the ice on a large lake about a quarter of a mile from the house would scare me. This cracking of the ice would happen particularly in a long stretch of severely cold weather. The water pressure cracking the ice as the ice gets thicker. When it cracked it sounded like the discharge of a high-powered rifle and the bullet glancing off something hard causing it to sling.

At 2 A.M. I would once more fill the stove with wood, give it a start, then shut the draft and retire. About 6 A.M. the man of the house would get up to do the firing.

I slept at the head of the stairs. The lady of the house gave me a small woolen shawl to drape around my hair-thinning head. It kept me nicely warm but all around the edge closest to my breathing apparatus was a ring of frost when I woke up in the morning. Is it necessary to tell what time that was? Let it suffice to say it was not six or seven o'clock. Well, the weather was "brrr" cold. Yes, it was! One night we left about a quarter cup of tea in a real "tea cup." The next morning it was frozen and the cup was cracked. When standing with the back toward the stove which was only a few feet away, the back was more than warm but that same person's breath could be seen. That is true. That large room we used was truly air conditioned. Jack Frost was a steady visitor.

Forenoon and afternoon I would have instruction periods with their son. I also gave him time to study.

I also had Sunday School with the other children and on several Sundays conducted worship services to which neighbors — they were few in the bush — were invited. Some did come. Services were held in the home where I stayed.

For exercise I carried firewood into the house; lots of it. Also chopped and split some. Then I would take the dapple grey stallion out of the barn, lead him down to the lake to water him and to give him some exercise. I had a large "circus ring" in the snow on the lake. I had a long rope tied to his halter. I stood in the middle and made him run around and around in this "circus ring." For watering the horses and cattle, a hole was kept open in the ice.

Before I left there we were out of firewood. That meant going into the bush and hauling some to the house. I helped do that. It also had to be sawed into stove-length blocks. This we did with a hand saw. I also helped do that.

About the end of January I confirmed the son. I did not get in contact with any of the other children of the original class I had on the prairie because they were too scattered and too far away and, also, the weather would not permit it. We did, however, make an attempt.

I left there on February 2nd. After a long ride in the "house" on sleigh runners, I boarded the train and headed for home by way of North Battleford and Saskatoon to Harris where we lived at the time. When the train arrived in North Battleford, the weather had become so mild that water was running between the tracks and there were water puddles on the roads. This was a chinook.

In North Battleford I had to change trains again. I knew that the illiterate but knowledgeable Christian and mission-minded man and his family from the prairie were living in the area. I had written them. He came to take me to the place where they lived. It was on a road allowance but the road was not going through there. When they left the prairie, they left in their cook wagon. This was a kitchen on wheels used by threshing crews. Parking on a roadway, they were considered "squatters." They had a few cows and a few horses, and most of the necessities needed in the cook wagon. They were very poor yet very happy in Christ, the Savior. I had a wonderful visit with them, discussing Scripture and singing a few hymns and praying together. They eventually landed in Olds, Alberta. They and we kept in contact with each other by an annual Christmas letter all these years.

Years later when we visited our daughter and family living in Calgary, we would also stop for a few hours to visit with this family. Olds was only a few miles off our highway.

They had a small house, were still living in poverty, but were active doing mission and church work. Fortunately for them, the little town of Olds had a Lutheran church. The Lord took the illiterate man to heaven several years ago but his wife, as far as I know, is still living in Olds, Alberta. We have not seen her for some years now — our daughter does not live in Calgary anymore — but have had a Christmas card from her each year with the usual letter until a year or two ago.

Oh, but I must get back to North Battleford to get back home to Harris; and I did. But when I had the door unlocked, I still could not get the door open far enough to get in. Due to the very cold weather we had had, the congoleum floor covering had curled up. All I could do was use force and break it off. I did. Home sweet home, but oh so cold and even "lonesome-er!" My family was still at Grandma's house in the U.S.A.

While building a fire in the kitchen stove my feet got colder and colder. They were warm when I entered the house. I warmed one room at a time and all I needed was the kitchen and a bedroom. I used the kitchen also for my study room. That was my trip into the bush and the experiences as I remember them.

Shortly after I was home, two men who were members of a preaching station I had about eight or ten miles east brought a load of fire wood. I had to open the basement window for them so they could unload it into the basement and I stayed down there to throw the wood away from the window. All at once it came to my mind that I had put a pair of shoes into the oven to warm them. My feet, as I wrote above, were cold and getting colder while I was building the fire. I rushed up and found my shoes done to a crisp with the toe of each shoe nicely curled up. Well, they were done all right! "Done for!"

Another time when I left to serve some of my preaching stations, I had forgotten to empty our drinking water pail. It was frozen solid with the dipper in it when I came back home. I had a good fire going in the cook stove. It was red hot, almost white hot. The pail with the solid block of ice I had set toward the back of the stove. After some time I wanted to pour some of the water from the partly melt ice into the teakettle which also was setting at the back end of the stove. As I was pouring I had hold of the dipper to make sure the ice would not slide out. Suddenly the dipper came loose from the ice and there it went — the ice — across the red hot stove. What a cloud of steam, but no water on the floor! I was sure the stove would be cracked or warped. I looked closely. No harm was done. That is life without a wife. Moral: Men, get a wife!

When spring came, not only did the birds, ducks, and geese come back, but so did my wife and two girls. But now my wife had to have her operation to have her goiter removed. This was a serious and particular operation. Our doctor sent her to a specialist in Winnipeg, Manitoba. There she spent a few days, while tests were made, with the family of a classmate of mine. The operation, thank God, was a complete success. In time she became her real self again. Many times she remarked that she certainly is glad and thankful that she had the goiter removed.

Our two little girls were with a family on a farm at one of my preaching stations. This family had three girls all older than our girls — ours were three and five — and they received more than enough attention and good care. But their daddy was "batchin' it again" except when at the various preaching stations. In the meantime, I also got most of the garden taken care of.

After my wife returned from Winnipeg a healthy woman again, everything in our household was running smoothly for about two years. Then the Board of Missions disturbed the quiet waters in our family life and rocked the boat a little by informing me that I was to be transferred to Lloydminster where I was to start building a congregation from scratch. Some pages back I already wrote about Lloydminster and what was taking place there — gas and oil had been discovered. So here I pick up the "moving thread" again which I promised I would do a number of pages back.

First of all it meant I had to inform my parish and then bring my service and work in the Rosetown parish, where I had many truly wonderful and pleasant experiences — also a few of the other kind — to a close on a pleasant note. But how does one do that when one has learned to love the people of the parish and they don't want you to leave them? But many had left me by moving north and so the people who stayed on the prairie understood, which made saying not "good-bye" but "farewell, God be with you and keep you in His grace and love" much easier.

About a year and a half after one of my preaching stations had moved north, I received a letter from the family in the bush, the family that took me to that "invisible" turkey dinner, whose son I instructed and confirmed while staying with them in the bush. Their letter was a request that I perform the wedding of the girl whose stillborn baby I had buried after helping dig the grave to keep from freezing to death. I told about this unforgettable experience some pages back.

It was in fall, I know; possibly the latter part of October, if my memory is still functioning correctly. It was a year before our move to Lloydminster. I did not want to go alone. Weather and roads could get bad at this time of the year in northern Canada. I don't remember whether or not I had any correspondence with those people up in the bush before I decided to go or not to go.

This girl, not a young girl, a little retarded but a good worker, was staying with the family whose son I confirmed in the bush. This family had moved to another place. I had the information how and where to find them. I discussed this matter with a member of a preaching station where I conducted a worship service about a week or ten days after receiving the letter. My family was with me. We stayed the night at this member's home every time I served this station. It was the same family that kept our girls while my wife was in Winnipeg for her operation. After discussing the matter with him, we decided I should go and he would go with me. I must have had some information on how to get in contact with the people in the bush because I can remember doing some phoning. This family where we were staying had a phone. My wife and girls stayed there while the member and his pastor went on a "wild goose chase." And that it was! You will agree when you have finished reading about this experience I had in Canada, the Land of Adventure and Promise.

Well, pastor and "one people" were on their way. I believe I still had my first "deluxe Chevy sedan." I do remember that I had my double barrel 12-gauge shotgun with me. I always carried that with me during hunting season. And I knew there were some good tasting grouse in the bush; perhaps I would get a chance to take a shot at some, or at some mallard ducks or Canada geese. If I remember correctly, that part of our trip was a "wild goose chase."

Without trouble, we arrived at the home of the people the girl was staying with. The good lady of the house provided us with something for our stomachs. But where is the girl? After visiting for some time, I asked about her. "She is getting cleaned up and will be out soon," the lady of the house informed me. Quite some time elapsed but she made no appearance. So I asked again. The lady of the house went to see what was delaying her. In a short time both appeared. After some discussion, I was confused, not knowing yet when, where, and even whether there was to be a wedding.

While there, I learned that the girl's parents also had come up into the bush. They were with a son a number of miles away. They wanted to see me. So, once this far, I might as well go a little farther. In the course of time I learned that there was to be no wedding but that the parents and a younger son "desperately" desired to get back to the prairie and asked whether I would take them along back. I was boiling inside but just did not have the heart to refuse to take them along. So we packed their few belongings into the car, which left little room for the three of them, and what we could not get into the car, including the little boy's wagon — what should we do with it? How can we take it all? Well, we hurriedly built a rack which we set on the gas tank at the back of the car. Cars had no trunks in those days. We fastened this rack with some rope some which way — I don't remember how; but I do remember we had to stop several times on the way home to "redo" what we had done. I never did get to meet the groom if there was such a thing in the bush.

On the way home but while still in the bush, I saw some grouse on the trail ahead of us; but I did not stop to shoot any. By this time I could not see straight anymore and would just have wasted my ammunition. I do not even remember anymore whether we stopped to eat anywhere. It was night by the time we arrived at the place where our "hitchhikers" wanted to go. We hurriedly unloaded them and theirs and were on our way to my member's home where my family was staying. On our way to his home we discussed our trip and came to the conclusion that the whole thing was a hoax to get me up there so that the girl's parents could get back to the prairie. I don't even remember whether I was remunerated for making this trip or not, except that the good Lord always does in one way or another for helping those in need. Even then, Reader, you must agree it was a "wild goose chase," eh?

* * * * * *

We were about to make the last move we made in Canada. But just how did we move? I have a lapse of memory on that. I asked my wife and she does not remember — and that is worse. All I can write is that we moved to Lloydminster the middle of October. The roads and weather were bad — rain, snow, sleet. How is it possible to forget *how* we moved?! But we *did* move.

The little house we had rented was quite crowded when our modest second-hand furniture was in it. But we managed. Even found room for an old Indian who came to our house once a year for several years to beg for a pot of tea, ginger (which he put into the tea), and for some food. He even stayed the night several times.

Installation was to take place the first Sunday in November. That meant several free Sundays for me. A small congregation at Artland, about 40 miles south of Lloydminster, had signed the call I received. In the meantime I made a goodly number of mission calls, some sick calls in the hospital, and also special calls on a few Lutheran families I was told about. This information I received from one of the families I had at Sibbald ("Jerusalem") who had moved to Blackfoot, Alberta, eight miles west of Lloydminster several years before I moved to Lloydminster. I had found a total of seven confirmed Lutherans. The first Sunday after I was installed, I began holding services on Sunday afternoon, three Sundays per month, in a Baptist church which I rented. There was no other time we could use the church and on the fourth Sunday I was out of town serving other stations. More about that later. The first service in Lloyd was held the second Sunday in November with an attendance of 26.

Now about being installed. The same man, the District Field Secretary, officiated again. It took place on the first Sunday in November in a congregation that was not even mentioned as being a part of my parish.

This was at Medstead about sixty or more miles northeast of Lloydminster. There was a group of people who had come to Canada from the Third German Reich. To be installed as their pastor made me quite unhappy. They had been served before as part of another parish, but the pastor of that parish accepted a call to another parish and that congregation was being added or had been added to my new parish without my knowledge. What does a young missionary do but submit and accept the situation.

I, of course, had to drive my car to this place. The roads were none too good because of the rain and snow we had had. And no roads were graveled except the very main highways. We drove to Medstead on Saturday.

After the installation service we went to the home of a member for a lunch — there was no reception after the service. There was no church building. We used the German Hall. The Field Secretary chats and visits and chats some more; and we were to get to Artland yet, 40 miles south of Lloydminster, for another installation service in the evening and it had snowed again Saturday night. The road was very slippery. We slid into the ditch several times but managed somehow to get out again — at least I do not remember that we were pulled out any time. Going was slow and the Field Secretary wanted me to drive a little faster. When I did, we slid from one side of the road to the other and, therefore, got down into the ditch several times. So I just drove a little slower and managed to move ahead and keep out of the ditch.

It was getting late afternoon and we still had a long way to go. When we arrived it was long past service time. No people at the school house where the service was to be held. We drove to a member's home, an elderly German couple, where we stayed the night. People were informed that the service would be held on Monday. I don't remember whether in the afternoon or evening. Possibly in the evening because we did not get back to Lloydminster until Tuesday. This was a trip of 191 miles and was not too pleasant. The Field Secretary left on the morning Canadian National sometime between 4:00 and 5:00 A.M.

I continued canvassing Lloydminster and area to find people I might win for Christ and His Kingdom. But I also had several other preaching stations in the parish to serve which previously were part of another parish and now also Medstead which, in the first place, was not a part of my parish but became part of my parish for about a year.

The Medstead congregation probably was the largest in the parish. I served them at least twice a month. Attendance at times was nearly fifty people. Among this group of Germans was a man who had been a teacher of religion in Germany but he did not attend the worship services. I called on him and spoke to him about it. But I got nowhere. I told him that God says that we are not to neglect the assembling of ourselves together, that He wants us to hear His word and worship Him in the congregation. I asked him how he would justify his disobedience of God on Judgment Day. He said: "Just let me take care of that, which I will be able to do. So you just let me alone. That is what I told the pastor before you came and we got along just fine." Some time later I visited him again with the elders. He told us the same thing. Our visits bore no fruit.

As I wrote pages back, I scheduled festival services in such a way that every station in the parish would, in the course of several years, have a service on the day of the festival. Medstead being the largest congregation in the parish, I scheduled Easter service with Holy Communion there for my first Easter in the new parish. My announcement of an Easter service with communion met with strenuous objections. I was dumbfounded! The reasons given were that the next day, Easter Monday, the Catholic people celebrated the end of their fasting during Lent here in this hall with a dance and a few other things and all of the Lutheran people here took part in that and to go to Communion the day before is just simply out of order and they would not have it. I tried to show them how wrong and sinful it all was but I did not get very far because one man jumped up on the stage and told me in no uncertain terms that I could not have Easter service and communion under those circumstances. Calmly I asked him what was more important to the people — celebrating the end of the Catholic fasting or celebrating the victory of Jesus over sin, death, and the devil, and partaking of the Lord's Supper for the assurance of forgiveness and eternal life? Others then said that they would not be attending my services. I said, "There will be no Easter service for you." I did not return for services until four weeks later. Their Catholic friends were also Germans and so I was convinced that these people were more German than Christian and more for Hitler and the Third German Reich than for Canada, where they were given a home after their homeland was badly devastated in World War I.

When I returned four weeks later, I conducted services but without communion. Not all of the people agreed with the majority. I stayed there an extra day to make some pastoral calls and also some mission calls with the idea of beginning English worship services in a school house. I could not think of holding English services in the hall. Four weeks later I returned and held a German service with communion in the morning and English services in the afternoon. Attendance at each was almost equal, about 30. I continued conducting English services and some of the Germans also came. I also taught Sunday School after the English service.

During the winter I used the train. I well remember when I walked from the home of the people where I stayed the night to the home of the people who were going to take me back to town to catch the train. The Medstead congregation, by the way, was a country congregation. Medstead was only a village. The people I stayed the night with told me just how or where to go to take a shortcut to the home of the people who were to take me to the train. I had my club-bag with my gown, and books to carry and a heavy overcoat — cowhide — which I wore. My father-in-law gave it to me. I had to walk about two miles. But I had to go through a bush area and that was difficult. It was around noon but there was no sunshine. Before long I was lost, not knowing what direction I was going. Believe me, that is an awful feeling! I walked and walked, getting deeper into the bush or walking in a big circle. I finally came upon a cow trail. I followed it, knowing it would lead me out. It did. I came to a fence at the end of the bush but could see no buildings. I climbed up the fence and could see a haystack and part of a building. But is that the place where I was to go? "It is for right now," I said to myself, feeling much better but a little "bushed." I followed the fence and when I came to the place, I soon learned that I was in the right place. Before long I was on my way to the depot and, once again, our good and gracious God brought me safely back home to my family.

Oh! during these escapades something wonderful happened in our family. Another cute little girl came to live with us. She arrived on February 3rd. We were happy to have her live with us. She was a "decided" brunette. So was girl No. 1; but girl No. 2 was a "decided" blond. We gave girl No. 3 the melodious name Alvina Aleta. One man said, when he heard what we called her: "I would not give my dog that name." But when I had the joy of baptizing her, her name was also written in the Book of Life and is still there for she, too, is still a true believer and is serving her Lord and Savior in the church.

Before writing about happenings at other places in my new parish, I shall finish telling of other experiences I had at Medstead during the short time I served there.

The congregation had arranged a meeting to be held after the first service I conducted there after the Easter service with communion to which they had objected. The objection was not to the Easter service but to communion because the next day they intended to celebrate with their Catholic friends who were celebrating because they were done with their Lenten fasting. At this meeting a man was present who did not attend church with his fellow German Lutherans but who claimed membership. He was really a mocker and was very outspoken and opened his mouth quite far against me at this meeting. I did not reply to his remarks. What they had hoped to accomplish in this meeting they did not accomplish, but they did let off some steam. I did not change my stand. It was the mocker, I believe, who wanted the meeting and had talked the elders into calling a meeting.

Not many weeks later, Christ, the Head of the church, arranged the opportunity for them to fulfill what they had hoped to accomplish in that meeting. The gentleman who had been a teacher of religion in Germany became ill. He was taken to a hospital where he died. Now, who was to conduct the funeral service? My phone rang; it was one of the elders. I was asked to bury this man but I had not been asked to visit him while he was ill in the hospital. I told the elder that I would not conduct the funeral service. I reminded him of the time the elders and I called on him and of the man's attitude and of what he had said, namely, that I was to let him alone, that he would settle with God himself. "No," I said, "I will not come."

There was an American Lutheran Church pastor in a town not far away. They tried to call him but he was not at home. They called me again. I repeated my answer which I had given before. "But, Pastor," they pleaded, "we want a German funeral service. The only pastor here is Methodist and he can not preach German."

"In that case," I said, "you will have to have an English funeral service. Just ask him. He will take the funeral. They bury anybody and everybody. I will not come, not even for the German you want." Then I hung up.

A week or ten days later I received a letter from the congregation in which I was denounced and told not to return. It was signed by, I believe, all male members and one or two who were not members but who were Germans, including the mocker. I immediately informed the Board of Missions in detail, including what had led up to this action on the part of the congregation. A meeting was scheduled to be held about a month later which was conducted by the District Field Secretary. The meeting was attended by only five men, which was something the Field Secretary could not understand. Oh, yes, I was present, but not one of the five. In the course of the discussion, which I shall not give details of, it became clear what led up to this letter I had received, who really were the instigators, and who went from home to home and got the men to sign it. One of them was the mocker. The five men present at the meeting confessed that they were not told all the details in the letter and had no idea that they signed something that led to this. They also said that had they known what they knew then, they would not have signed it. They likewise expressed their regrets and sorrow. But the deed was done. The Field Secretary just could not believe and understand that these German Lutheran people would do such a thing. This he repeated several times. I guess he just did not "read" them right. Not once did he say anything against me, but rather upheld me. The five men who were present truly let their Christian friendliness toward me shine through.

The majority of the people and those who wrote and sent the letter but who were not present at the meeting were the people who wanted to get rid of me — and they did — but who had not expected the District to let them down and to sever its connections with them. That closes the book on Medstead.

In between time when I had all these experiences at Medstead, I was kept really busy making mission calls especially in Lloydminster, hospital calls, teaching confirmation classes in several places, preparing sermons, etc. In Lloydminster I tried to have three services every month but did not always succeed because of other preaching stations that also called for my attention. My parish consisted of nine preaching stations by now. Before the end of 1940 I added one more when the Board of Missions of the Alberta-British Columbia District asked the Board of Missions of the Manitoba-Saskatchewan District to add a preaching station 40 miles northwest of Lloydminster to my parish because it was closer to Lloydminster than to any parish in their district. So now I had a parish of ten preaching stations from 40 miles west of Lloydminster to 100 miles east of Lloydminster. As much as possible, I served three stations every Sunday except in winter and seldom preached less than three times, often four times and sometimes five times, in a week, especially in winter. Besides that, I had confirmation classes at various stations, adults as well as children.

The Lloydminster preaching station, of course, received special attention and slowly, but surely, was gaining in membership. Also, a few more families from "Jerusalem" on the prairie had moved up into this beautiful and fertile country. Will write a little more about that country later.

By the end of 1939 the Lloydminster preaching station became an organized congregation and called themselves First Lutheran Church of Lloydminster, Saskatchewan. Throughout the parish, attendance ranged from 12 to 50, sometimes 60. Offerings still were small because of the depression which, however, had not been as severe here as further south on the prairie. Conditions, however, were improving as the drought and windy years were at an end. One experience I had the second year (1937) I was at Lloydminster is another unforgettable one. All of a sudden I became a grain buyer. The dairyman-member I had at Rosetown needed feed badly for his Holstein milk cows. They had no crop on the prairie. In our area there was a fairly good oats crop and he begged me to buy and load and ship him a carload of oats. I consulted one of my farmer members, the one who had come up there from "Jerusalem" a year or two before I had. He was willing to help me; in fact, he did most of the buying and work. He made arrangements with one of the elevator operators in Blackfoot, Alberta, about 8 miles west of Lloyd, to let us load it through his elevator at so much per bushel or pound. He agreed to do that. When it was loaded and shipped and the dairyman unloaded it, he wrote that he was very satisfied. He said it was the best measure in his favor he had ever received and he was also very happy with the quality of the oats. The farmers were also satisfied with the price paid them.

My memory does not tell me what he paid me and my "side-kick" for the work, but I am sure he did pay us. If he had not, isn't that what a person would remember? So he must have.

September and part of October of 1937 we spent at the homes of the two Grandmas and Grandpas in Nebraska. We had a good trip both ways that time. Wonder what make of second-hand car I had then. I don't remember. A Maxwell?

Not very long after we had arrived in Lloydminster, maybe six months after, the couple I already wrote about who lost two infants while on the prairie, the couple who began the track north with the people of the preaching station where they were members but turned back again, finally moved further north also. They settled in the Battleford area, the extreme east end of my parish. (Battleford, by the way, was once the headquarters of the famous Northwest Mounted Police. This headquarters is now Mounted Police Museum.)

Well, one day while this couple was on their way to Battleford in their lumber wagon, the only means of conveyance they had at that time, spied a part of a newspaper in the ditch along the road. They stopped to pick it up. They had had no newspaper for quite some time. In it the lady read the news item that Pastor H. Brase had been transferred from Rosetown to Lloydminster. They came to Lloydminster to look us up. I don't exactly remember how they got there. Not by lumber wagon, this I know. I believe a neighbor of theirs had a car and had to make a trip to Lloydminster and they came with him. They went to a grocery store and asked where we lived. The purpose of their visit was to find out how close to Battleford I had a preaching station. I do not remember whether I had already started a preaching station near Battleford or not. Hardly! But I soon thereafter started one there. Somehow I discovered a few more Lutheran families about ten or twelve miles west of Battleford. We held the services in various homes and — especially in the summer — in several school houses. The Battle River somewhat divided our preaching station. So, to be fair to all, if that is poossible, we held services in the summertime once north of the river and the next time south of the river. This family who came to Lloydminster to call on us was on the south side of the river. So when we had services on the north side of the river, they had about 20 miles to come to church; but they never missed in spite of the fact that they had only a wagon to travel in and no bridge near to cross the river. They drove through the river which was not very big.

In the winter time when I had to travel by train to serve Battleford and the rest of the parish, I would get off at North Battleford. The North Saskatchewan River flowed between the two towns, of which North Battleford was the larger by far. Here I took another train — a mixed train — to Prongua. There was no direct train connection between the two Battlefords. Prongua was west and a little south of Battleford and the preaching station was in the country west of Battleford and some north. If the train was not too late I would arrive at Prongua about the middle of the forenoon.

I boarded the first train in Lloydminster somewhere near 5:00 A.M. I would fasten my ticket to the shade on the window for the conductor to get and I would curl up in my seat to snatch about three hours of sleep — maybe. The train man would wake me just before we arrived at North Battleford. Only once I went right back to sleep. The train stopped here about 20 minutes. It was a divisional point. When I finally woke up, the train was on its way out of town. I hurriedly asked the conductor to stop the train and let me off. He did and as I remember it, or I better say if I remember correctly, he even had the train back up to the station during which time he gave me a short lecture which I can not repeat.

All went well! I still got on the mixed train to Prongua. When we arrived in Prongua, there was my faithful Christian man to meet me and take me to his home for breakfast. Then we would visit, discussing Scripture texts which they had listed and wanted to ask about. They also were faithful listeners to The Lutheran Hour and supported The Lutheran Hour regularly in spite of their poverty. The lady of the house also took the Bible course offered by The Lutheran Hour.

After the noon lunch we would go to wherever the service was scheduled to be held. When communion would be celebrated in this preaching station, registration would be taken just before the service began and all I had to do was write down the names of those that were absent, which was seldom. As a rule all I had to write was "All." After the service they always served a lunch which people brought during which "profitable" visits and discussions were carried on.

The night I would spend with the people who met me at the train. The evening was spent in discussing Bible passages or religious topics which often lasted into the early morning hours. Oh, what wonderful and inspiring hours they were! Never shall I forget them! But a good thing was that my train did not return until the afternoon. And the bad thing was that on my way home I had to wait four to six hours and sometimes longer for the change of trains in North Battleford. I arrived home, as a rule, after midnight, sometimes two hours after midnight, and then walked home five or six blocks in the bitter cold. But that did not subtract anything from the wonderful hours I spent with those people discussing the saving word of our gracious God.

The "house" those people lived in! The head of the family built it himself. He cut poles from poplar trees on his place, three to six inches in diameter, set them upright into the ground like posts but one next to the other. Two rooms, and a lean-to kitchen. The roof also was poplar poles. Then he mudded the walls and tacked some paper and cardboard over it. The roof he covered with straw and hay. I do remember that it leaked when it rained. But the room was rather small — the rest I will leave to your imagination. My clothes, however, I managed to keep in the dry. Yet I would not trade the wonderful experiences and profitable hours I had in the home of these and many other people there for anything in the world.

This preaching station was 100 miles from Lloydminster so also in the summer I usually stayed overnight with this family. It was the third place I served on a Sunday. That is why I was there also when it rained and not only when it snowed.

This family with one son was the poorest family — financially — that I ever had in any parish, but they always supported the church as well as The Lutheran Hour and I often wondered how it was possible for them. Of course, they did get some relief from the government, but so did nearly everybody else during the depression of the 30's.

One more story I must tell about this family. They always kept one dollar on reserve in case of an emergency, like sickness. So it happened: the lady of the house caught a bad cold and had a severe cough. Her husband took the dollar, drove into town, and bought a bottle of cough medicine. In those days one could get a bottle of cough medicine for less than a dollar. He gave the merchant the dollar. The merchant went to his till and came back with change for a ten dollar bill. The man said: "You made a mistake. I gave you a one dollar bill." "No, you did not. You gave me a ten dollar bill. I can prove it. I had no ten dollar bill in the till but have now." Then he went and showed it to the man who bought the cough medicine. The man replied: "I know it was a one dollar bill because we had it for a long time. We saved it for an emergency like this." The man took the change and medicine and went home. He told me this story several times and strongly believes that God performed a miracle, changing the one dollar bill into a ten dollar bill when the merchant took it to get the change. Yes, there is nothing impossible with God and He does truly great things His wonders to perform.

A last word about this family. They are now living in retirement, quite comfortably, in Saskatoon, Saskatchewan, in a place for senior citizens where each couple has a separate dwelling with ample room. Here they may live as long as they are able to take care of themselves. When we go to Lloydminster to visit our daughter and her family, we always stop to visit these elderly people. They are still in fair health except the lady is becoming very shaky. But they are happy, go to church regularly, and have their trust and hope in Jesus Christ, their Lord God and Savior. Oh, yes, a small garden goes with the dwelling place, which they make good use of.

There are other unforgettable experiences I had in this preaching station. One that I remember is when I was instructing the two grown-up boys of a Scandinavian family in their hone and I fell asleep while instructing them. It was rather embarrassing but I was just completely worn out from all the traveling, especially from the lack of sleep because of the early hour in the morning that I had to get up to catch my train. Then I would ride in a sleigh six to ten miles (it was winter when I fell asleep during class), and often I would run behind the sleigh to keep warm. Then when in a warm room, I just did not have enough energy left to keep my eyes open. But it was only for a moment and I was awake again long enough to excuse myself, dismiss the class, and ask if I could lie down for a nap. They understood for they knew that I was home very little and when I was home I had to prepare sermons and also had other work to do.

I gave little of my time to my children, which I regret to this day. They did not really learn to know their father as a father, mostly only as a man who came to their house for a few days to fill the tank we had in the house with snow for soft water, to haul water from the town well to fill the crock with drinking water, to then get cleaned up, put on clean clothes, and to go away again. But we did go to one of the lakes not far away for a week or so during the summer to do some fishing.

Oh, those good Jack fish and pickerels! And did we eat fish while at the lake! Deep, clear, cold water fish from the hook into the frying pan. Mmm! Mmm! Good! And one summer after eating our fill and then some, we still had 90 pounds of clean fish ready for the frying pan to take home and put into a locker at the butcher shop. Any fish eight inches or less in length we had to throw back into the lake. We caught fish anywhere from three to fifteen pounds — and that is no "fish story." Neither is this one: We caught two fish on one hook at the same time. Impossible?! Oh, no! You see, a good sized fish — possibly 18 to 20 inches long — had swallowed a smaller fish — possibly 10 to 12 inches long — and the tail end of that fish was still sticking out of that "Jonah"-fish's throat which we saw when we took the hook out of the "Jonah"-fish's mouth.

At another time we had an orphan girl staying with us who was a waitress in one of the Chinese restaurants. We took her to the lake with us. I was rowing the boat. She put the hook, line, and sinker over the side of the boat and the hook was hardly in the water when a nice big Jack fish went for it and landed right in the boat and did not even have the hook caught in his mouth. And that is NOT a "fish story!" You, dear Reader, may repeat either one without apology or blushing.

Now, as I promised, I shall write a little about the country we were now living in. It is beautiful country, and has fertile, black soil, especially at Lloydminster. This is what is known as the Park Belt area with many bluffs, some small and some quite large, of mostly poplar trees and some birch. There is also some wild fruit, such as Saskatoon berry, wild raspberry, wild strawberry, choke cherry, and pin cherry. Also, there are some smaller lakes not good for fishing but for wild ducks and geese during hunting season. Yes, I did some hunting when or if I had time.

The main crop was wheat but it was good oats country also and we had the oats king of the world in this area for quite a few years. The country is what you might call "rolling," not "hilly" nor flat country.

The soil at Lloydminster was the best soil for a garden that we ever had. Nowhere did we ever have potatoes, peas, carrots, and any other vegetables like we had there. We did not have to use insecticides at all. Our cauliflower was as white as snow and as large as a dinner plate. But sweet corn we seldom had and only few tomatoes ripened on the vine. In fall we would cover the tomato plants for a while at night; but when the danger of frost was great, we picked them, packed them in boxes, and put some under the stove and the others under the bed. We also had a most beautiful lawn, so thick that my reel-type mower would at times slide because it could not cut all the grass except when I would pull and push it back and forth in short fast strokes. And for a background to the lawn, we had a sweet pea fence about twelve or fifteen feet long covered with thousands of blooms of all colors, even though we picked several bouquets every day.

Our vegetable and flower garden was not perfect every year because of late frost or early frost, and one year I remember we had some frost every month of the year. But I also remember that one year we had no frost until the middle of November, what that meant for the gardens you can well imagine. Peas kept on bearing, as they always did, until they were killed by frost. The good gardens and the canning my good cook did made a big difference in the grocery bills. Of course, our salary had gone up some by this time after about ten years in the ministry. Oh, by the way, salary was increased five dollars per month for every child that was added to the family up to four children. After that mom and dad were on their own, and we were getting ready to welcome daughter number four, and the five dollar raise as well. The day this happened was November 29, 1938. The rhythmic name we gave her was Cordelia Marlene, which was also written in the Book of Life when she was baptized and God washed away her sins and received her into His family as His child. In the 17th year of her life He took her to Himself into the glorious heavenly home when her life was ended very abruptly in a car accident at the front steps of the church I was then serving near Omaha, Nebraska. She had gone to a neighbor's home to watch television. Ten o'clock or a little after the neighbor's son brought her home in his pickup. At the crossroad a car which ran the stop sign hit the pickup broadside and killed our fourth daughter. The young man was slightly injured. This was in 1956.

Now back to the 30's and the Lloydminster parish in which I had more to do than I could do justice to. I put in many hours as well as made some extra trips to the various stations teaching adults as well as children in the chief parts of Christian doctrine in preparation for confirmation in the faith and for communicant membership in the church. Among the adults were also such who had never been baptized, which was administered when they were confirmed. I was home with my family seldom more than 12 to 15 days a month. At times I was gone ten days in succession, especially when I was also taking care of a vacant parish. Then I would come home for a day or two and be gone again. In summer I would take the family along quite often.

I also conducted Bible Class in the evening at several places, particularly for young people. I had organized a Young People's Society in Lloydminster and they spent most of their meetings in the study and discussion of the Bible. At times they carried these meetings on till late and I would have to tell them to close because it was time for them to go home. Bible Class was held in our home. Even during lunch time they kept on discussing Scripture. It was truly and remarkably and pleasingly wonderful. One would think that some at least would drop out sooner or later but that was not the case. Even a number of parents began coming and a few who had no young people.

In Edmonton, 160 miles west of Lloydminster, our Synod has one of its Concordia Colleges for teaching and training young men in preparation for the office of the ministry. All the boys were not able to go home for Christmas because of the lack of sufficient money for travel. Some people closer by would go get one or two of the boys and take them into their home for the Christmas holidays.

We did this one Christmas. I then took the young man with me on my trips to a few of my preaching stations. One instance I will never forget. I wanted to conduct a Christmas service at a station about 20 miles northeast of Lloydminster. We got about half way and then we got stuck in a snow drift. We shoveled ourselves out several times but now saw that the road was badly drifted for quite a distance ahead and we were running late. We decided we could not make it through the drifts ahead of us and still get there on time. So we turned around and headed for home. On our way home we came by a farm place where a family lived that I had heard about. They were churchless but had been shopping around for a church.

They came from Holland. I turned into their lane and said to the student: "Now you shall see a missionary in action." We were received with joy. My wife was also with us. (We had someone to stay with our girls at home.) It was a most pleasant visit and even more successful. Their oldest daughter was immediately enrolled in the confirmation class, the parents too would take instructions later, and they had another girl and three boys. None of the boys were baptized. All were enrolled in Sunday school that day. They found what they were looking for in the Lutheran Church. They came to church regularly from that day on.

Toward spring I went to their home regularly to instruct the parents. Wheat-seeding time came before we were through. I suggested we take a break so he could get his seeding done. But he would not hear of it. He said: "No, this is more important, and I will get the seeding done also." So we continued. Class was, of course, held in the evening in their home.

When we had concluded the indoctrination, I confirmed them in a public worship service as this is what they desired.

I also baptized the Mrs. and the three younger children. It was a truly happy day for them as well as for me and the congregation. The whole family attended the worship services absolutely regularly, also the Lenten services and the week-day Bible class. They supported the church with liberal contributions which somewhat "disturbed" me — if that is the right word to describe my feeling — because I was aware of their financial status. One day, maybe a year or longer after they became members of the church, the Mrs. called on me for some purpose which I do not remember anymore. But I do remember that they were by no means rich so I asked her how they could manage with their family, come to town at least four times a week and still support the kingdom of God so liberally. I also remember her reply. She said: "Pastor, since we joined the church and have given ourselves to the Lord, we are financially better situated than we ever were." What proof that is that we do not give ourselves poor if we first give ourselves to the Lord, trust in Him and His promises, and give out of love and gratitude to Him for all He has done for us and has given to us and daily gives us. And it also proves that God keeps His promises, as: "Give and it shall be given unto you." We cannot lose by gathering treasure in heaven. This also reminds me of what the Apostle Paul writes in the last verse of his mighty resurrection chapter, 1 Corinthians 15, namely that whatever we do for the Lord is never wasted or for nothing. Then in the next chapter, the second verse, he writes about giving and tells us how we are to do it. And remember, Paul is writing this by the inspiration of God, the Holy Spirit, so it is meant also for you and for me.

This family lived nine and one half miles from church in Lloydminster. Their place was one half mile off the highway, the only graveled road in the area in those days and which was kept open in winter. When that half mile was blocked by snow drifts, the father of the family would pull the car with the family in it to the highway with his horses. Then he would take the horses back home, return to the car on foot, and they would come to church. To get back home again he would reverse the order. Finally a neighbor living on the highway only a short distance from where this family entered the highway told him to put his horses into his barn. At times he would leave the car at the neighbor's place and use a sleigh to transport his family to and fro. Through such deeds of love for the Lord and such devotion on the part of God's people, God lets His servants see the fruits of their labors.

During the Second World War the father of this family received a call to duty to serve in the Dutch army in Canada. There seems to have been some kind of arrangement between the Dutch and Canadian governments. I know the Queen of Holland was in Canada for her safety. The man did not answer the first call. Then he received another call with a little "ginger" in it. He was to report in Ontario. So they had a farm sale and moved to Ontario. He served in the Dutch army as cook for the Queen. And you better believe it, God had His hand also in this. " . . . FOR HE IS GOOD . . . " After the war they made their permanent home in Ontario where they are still faithful to their Lord Christ and His church. We have annual contact with them by letter at Christmas time.

Just what moved me to turn into their place that day when we could not get through the snow drifts that I might deliver a Christmas message at one of my preaching stations? God did, Who works in a mysterious way His wonders to perform. He knew that there was good soil and the seed He privileged me to sow brought forth fruit a hundredfold.

Another unforgettable experience in Lloydminster was the joy of instructing and confirming a lady who was won for Christ and the church through the kindness and concern of a church member — a lady — who brought her to the worship services and then to Bible Class. I called on her and her family. Her husband was a confirmed Lutheran, confirmed in his youth in a Scandinavian Lutheran Church about twenty-five miles southwest of Lloydminster. When she was ready for confirmation in the faith, I also baptized their children. Five, if my memory is still functioning correctly. This family also was faithful to Christ and His church from then on. I remember this lady once asking me whether I know what really gave her the desire to become a member of our congregation. I, of course, did not know. She told me that it was the friendliness of the members of the church. Yes, how true! Christian love and friendliness is a strong magnet, drawing others into our association and so finally to Christ, the Savior. This family moved to Edmonton, Alberta, a few years later where they continued their church life. It was the man's work that moved them to Edmonton.

There are more such and similar happy experiences I could write about, but I believe I have given enough evidence that the Lord was causing the seed I was privileged to sow to spring up and bear fruit, some a hundredfold. But some sprang up and died again before bearing fruit because it fell on rocky soil or among weeds; and some fell on the hard path and did not even sprout. The congregation, however, under the Lord's blessing, grew larger and stronger.

* * * * * *

A year or so after moving to Lloydminster we found a little larger house. So we moved once more. But we still had only two bedrooms, but a basement under part of the house and a much larger yard and garden space. And it was much, much closer to the depot — not quite half the distance — which made quite a difference when it was cold and I had to get up at four in the morning and walk to the depot carrying a grip with all the books I needed. In a mission field, the preacher furnishes the books needed to conduct the service.

At several of the other preaching stations I also had some adults I was indoctrinating in preparation for church membership, especially at Artland, forty miles south of Lloydminster. Not to prolong the period of indoctrination too long, I made extra trips there during the week, not every week, because I also had some adults to indoctrinate at a few other preaching stations, especially at Battleford which was almost a hundred miles east of Lloydminster. How many hours in a week do you suppose I spent with my family of girls?

At Artland where I had only German services, I also began to conduct services in English, which almost doubled the attendance. This is what opened the door to the instruction of a number of adults. The children of some of the German people were now also instructed and confirmed in English.

One most unusual experience I had at Artland which is unforgettable is when the husband of one of the adults I had instructed in the chief parts of Christian doctrine came to me to excuse himself for being absent from church one Sunday. That is something unusual! Do you know of anyone that ever did that? I don't. This man's excuse was that he had set his alarm which woke him all right. But he was so tired that he did not get up at once. So he fell asleep again. When he woke up again, it was too late to go to church. This was during the threshing time. He was the thresher and wanted to finish a job at a farmer's place (it was Saturday) and so it got a little late he told me and then added, "I am ashamed and sorry that I was absent from worship." He had never been absent since he and his family began coming to church.

Something else that I shall never forget is when one of the German members at Artland gave me the advice never to preach about money and giving because most of the people (the Germans) do not want to hear about it. No doubt, dear Reader, you can guess what my next German sermon was about. His advice did tell me what I must do, not what I must avoid. God wants us to preach all of His Word, also what sinful people do not want to hear but need to hear. "All things whatsoever I have commanded you," Jesus said. These German people were not really poor, but were poor givers. They evidently realized it but did not want to be told or encouraged to give God His share of what He first of all gives them. And after being told and encouraged with the Gospel of Jesus' love, they did not respond with a greater measure of love to Him in their giving.

The congregation was in the country. Artland was a stop for every train on the Canadian National Coast to Coast main line because of a water tower there. (There were no diesel engines in those days.) Besides the "famous" water tower, Artland also had a grain elevator. Here at Artland is where our girls and I, and many other people, got to see and hear the King and Queen of England while the engine was given a big drink of good water. King George VI and his Queen Elizabeth, a most gracious lady, were visiting Canada at the time. The girls and I got within about twenty feet of them. But a person had to be careful not to be pushed over and trampled. Everybody wanted to get a "good" look at the pretty Queen. What a thrill! Once in a lifetime! My queen, however, is much prettier and that gives me a thrill which lasts not only for the time of a fill of water, but for a whole lifetime.

The first time I conducted a service at Artland after my installation in this new, and my last, parish in Canada, I stayed the night with an elderly German couple. Several years before this time they had built a fairly large addition to their little house they had lived in and were still living in. You will see why when you read about the experience I had the first time I stayed with them. The new part was well furnished: the large living room, dining room, bedroom, and veranda. If I remember correctly, it also had a second story.

When the pastor stays there, where does he sleep? In the new bedroom, of course. Oh, the weather was cold, and had been cold for some days. The room was cold. The bed was colder. The sheets felt as though I had just crawled between two blocks of ice. Even the feather tick did not help. (Dear Reader, if you do not know what a feather tick[†] is, ask Grandma. It is not related to a wood tick.)

I had very little, if any, sleep that night. Never was I so cold in bed. I had to keep moving and working to keep my blood from freezing into bloody icicles. Why did they not warm the room? The problem was, they had failed to build a chimney in the new addition. The new addition was rarely used, and then only in summer, depending on who was visiting the elderly couple.

At other places I had "a buggy time" sleeping. When I am given a bed for myself to sleep in, I don't expect company in bed. But at a number of places I did have company, undesirable company at that. The company would crawl all over me, but would not hurt me. There was not only one, but many — too many — and still undesirable company. I would get after them and when I would catch one, I would squeeze it to death, then smell my fingers, "phui," what an odor! And what smells so "phui-like" in death? Only the bedbug. I hated them, even though they did not bite me. One family I stayed with — no more often than I had to — slept in a granary in summer, but the pastor had to sleep in the house but was never alone in bed. In the winter the bedbugs do like the bears: hibernate.

I always wondered why bedbugs don't bite me and am still wondering. What is wrong with me? But my wife does not have that problem because they really love her and almost suck her dry of blood in one night.

At times my wife would go with me to a preaching station further away. A neighbor would be with our girls. One time we stayed all night with a young couple. They had only a small house, a shell really, but room for us. After we were in bed only a short time the bedbugs got busy on my wife, and there was a whole battalion. She tried to fight them off but it was a losing battle. She retreated to a bench in the kitchen where she tried to sleep until daybreak. I felt sorry for her. But I stayed

[†]A linen or cotton bag filled with feathers, sewn tightly shut, and often laid on top of a harder mattress for warmth and comfort.

with the bedbugs in bed. I hated the feeling of them crawling on me but finally did fall asleep and got up in the morning without a "bump" and unharmed. What lovely and considerate little creatures! But, oh, if I had had adenoids* and would have slept with my mouth open!

But poor wifey. She had a dozen or more *big* battle scars between her right elbow and shoulder and other places on her body. One eye was almost swelled shut and her upper lip was almost twice its normal size, or was it the lower lip? Well, whichever it was, she looked really "bumpy."

I must take you back to Rosetown for another "buggy" story. While living there we had bedbugs in our house. I had built a bed for our first daughter out of some crating which was made of some thin "veneer," I guess some would call it. The frame of the crate was built of 1" x 2" boards. But I could not use the same nail holes. After some time, the child would become very restless during the night. Mother would get up to quiet her. Before very long Mother noticed some "bumps" on our daughter. Mother wondered whether it could be bedbugs. She examined the bed but found nothing. The bugs hide when it is light. The next time the little one became restless, Mother got up, turned on the light, quickly threw the cover back, and there a bug was hurrying to a dark corner. Did the bugs come in the wood of the crate? Did I bring some home? Or where did they come from?

The next day I examined the whole bed, stuck a toothpick or match into the nail holes, smelled the stick, and that told me that we had undesirable company in the baby's bed. I went to a store to ask for something that would kill bedbugs. My wife objected to my procedure because she felt it was a disgrace to have bedbugs and now people would know. Well, a decision had to be made. I decided: disgrace does not bite a person, does not give him or her bumps, nor causes restless sleeping. Bedbugs do all of that and stink besides, but decisions don't. So I decided to have disgrace rather than bedbugs. The first store I stopped in, I was told to go to the hardware store. The man at the hardware store sold me what I needed and it worked. "Bye-Bye, Bedbugs" I could now sing. Yes, sirree, they were gone. About two weeks later when I brought home the mail and newspaper, what do you think I brought home in the newspaper besides the news and comic strips? Yep, you are correct: a beautiful bedbug. Of

*The patch of tissue that is high up in the throat, just behind the nose. They, along with the tonsils, are part of the lymphatic system.

all things, a newspaper including such an unusual gift. How did they know we were completely out of bedbugs? How considerate and generous of that editor! Could he spare one? Never did find out. So that remains just one more of the unsolved mysteries.

Now back to Lloydminster on a more pleasant note.

On our tenth anniversary — both in the ministry and in marriage — First Lutheran congregation in Lloydminster had a truly pleasant surprise for my wife and me. After a service the congregation gave us a mantle clock for our anniversary. It was a surprise in the full sense of the word: I never did find out how they knew. The clock still runs and strikes. So as the clock is still ticking and striking on and on, we have been and still are strikingly reminded of First Lutheran and its members again and again. And truly, fond memories they are!

But time had run out for an elderly lady and I must now tell you about my trip to the place of burial, about twenty or twenty-five miles southeast of Lloydminster. It was spring time. We had had quite a heavy snowfall in the winter, most of which was melted by this time. Water, water everywhere! A goodly number of the roads were under water. I could not get there by car. But there was a section foreman or worker on the Canadian Pacific Railroad who, I believe, was a friend of the family for whom I was to conduct the funeral service. The people concerned met me coming in on a handcar and then took me in a lumber wagon to the home where the funeral service was to be conducted. We drove through much water to get there. Arrangements had been made for me to get back to Lloydminster the same day but I do not remember whether it was by train or handcar. There was a train — a mixed train — once a week that came on a short side-line, made connection at the town to which I had been taken by handcar. Just how I got back to Lloydminster I do not remember anymore, but I do know that I got home. But how? My built-in computer is not functioning properly on this item. All I know for sure is that I buried the dead and, under God's gracious protection, arrived safely home again.

Hazeldine, Alberta, forty miles northwest of Lloydminster, I served once a month in winter and twice a month in summer. In the winter I went there by train. The train arrived about 9:00 A.M. I would then walk, carrying my grip with books and gown, to a member's home about a mile north of Hazeldine. If there was not too much snow it was not too bad, just good exercise to work up a good appetite for the breakfast I would get there. Often the boys were not up yet when I arrived but the lady of the house, who was a widow, was up. Early afternoon services were held in the homes of the members, just like the apostles did in the beginning of the New Testament Christian Church. There was something good about this: it brought about a closeness like in a family as we visited after the services over a cup of coffee and a sandwich.

During the summer services were held in the Hazeldine school house. Then the children could also be present and I would have a Bible Story Telling Period for them during the service — and I also made some applications for the adults. The Bible story would take the place of one of the Scripture readings, either the epistle or gospel lesson. After the service I had catechism recitations with the children. When the children were not present — as in winter — I did not tell a Bible story. The children were in school. So one time a few of the adults asked why I do not tell a Bible story when the children are not present. "We get more out of the Bible story than out of your sermon," they said. Hmmm! How was I to understand that? I believe they sensed my bewilderment. I was silent. Someone then added: "Oh, we don't mean to say your sermons are not good. It is just that the stories bring much back into our memory." Well, it is the Word of God as recorded in the Bible which is the power of God unto salvation to everyone who believes it. Therefore the apostles also wrote by inspiration: "Preach the Word, in season and out of season." "The word is able to save your soul." And Jesus prayed: "Sanctify them by Thy Truth. Thy Word is Truth." John 17:7.

At Hazeldine there was a lady and her daughter who I always picked up and took along to church when I was able to come by car. Then, of course, I also had to take them home again and did not mind doing this because I always "had" to stay for supper. And, oh, what a supper she served, always topped with a tremendous dessert. Delicious! During raspberry season it was raspberry Shortcake. The pieces of Shortcake were about 4" x 4" x 4" — at least they seemed to be — "as I remember it," and by the time the raspberries plus whipped cream — not a substitute but the real thing — were added, wow, what a "he-man-sized dessert." My daughters will vouch for that. They had the pleasure or misery of getting around such a supper and dessert occasionally when Dad would take them along. Since I do not get in on anything like that anymore, it does not surprise me that I came down to 125 pounds. While I was in Canada, the doctor, believe it or not, put me on a diet to cut down my weight. But I liked my diet. It was mostly vegetables, and mostly raw. You readers who see me now know I am not on that diet anymore. I am trying to gain a little and have even resorted to drinking "a beer" everyday, just about everyday. But no good! Guess I should go back to raspberry shortcake. But I have no raspberries and no cow.

"As I Remember It," a most unusual incident comes to mind and I wonder if any other pastor ever experienced anything like it. One day a man knocked at my door in Lloydminster who had a most unique request which he put before me. I was truly, as one says, "flabbergasted" and "as I remember it," I believe I did not even invite him into the house. You probably will understand that neglect or failure or stupid blunder on my part when I tell you what the he told me and requested of me.

This is his story and request "As I Remember It!" "My wife," he said, "has instructed a teenaged girl in Luther's Small Catechism." (They were Lutheran people living quite a distance from Lloydminster as well as from any Lutheran church and a means of conveyance was another problem. I must remind you this was during or right after the great depression of the 30's.) His request was: "Will you come to our home and examine the girl to determine whether she is indoctrinated well enough to be confirmed, and if so, will you confirm her?" I agreed to this. I do not remember how he found out about me nor whether the girl was baptized or not, but it seems to me that she was. We agreed on a date for the examination and confirmation. He gave me good directions to his home. My computer does not remember how many miles it was from Lloydminster. All I can remember is that it was quite a ways. But I do remember that she had been well instructed and passed her examination with flying colors. She also had been baptized. What a thrill that was for me, and what a lesson for you, my Christian friend, who is reading this. And I want to lay it upon your heart that it is not necessary that a pastor must in every case do the instructing but that you can do it and the matter of fact is, Jesus wants you to do it when He says: "Go ye and make disciples of all nations (all people), teaching them to observe all things whatsoever I Have commanded you." It is easier to get a person to listen to and receive instruction from a layman or laywoman in an informal setting than to get him or her to join a class. Think it over and try to visualize what joy you would have from such "disciple making" and what growth it would mean to God's Kingdom of grace. Right? Right!

Back to Artland once more. As time went on, some of the English speaking people moved away, also some of the German speaking, seeking greener pastures elsewhere. The young people sought work elsewhere. The Germans still there were irregular in their church attendance and did little in support of the church and its work. As the congregation became smaller and the people less interested and unwilling, the Board of Missions asked that services be terminated. When this decision was made known to the congregation, there was "as I remember it," no objection voiced.

That, with a few other smaller preaching stations eliminated, gave more time and opportunity for greater concentration in Lloydminster to build up the congregation in this rapidly growing "oil" town. A few of the families from the outlying preaching stations moved into Lloydminster, which helped much in building up our young congregation. The purpose of the smaller preaching stations near Lloydminster was to get people interested and to become feeders for the congregation in Lloydminster.

World war II was in full swing which created various difficulties and caused some problems, mostly because we were Lutherans — followers of Luther, who was a German, and some of our members were German, or at least of German descent. A few of them (but very few) naturally, but unfortunately, made remarks favorable to Hitler and Germany in our town which was founded by English settlers back in 1903. The remarks made by one or two put all of us under suspicion. Matter of fact, the town was named after a bishop of the Church of England (Anglican or Episcopal in the U.S.A.) whose name was Lloyd. At our residence we had "peeping Toms." Foot prints in the snow proved that. During the services held in the Baptist Church — where I also had conducted some services in the German language — we were being spied on by various people, including some of the town's officials. One of them called on the pastor of the Baptist church, told him we were conducting Nazi meetings, and asked him to forbid us the use of the church, which we were still renting. But that official was barking up the wrong tree and must have felt quite foolish when the pastor of the Baptist church replied: "You are mistaken, Mr. ??. I am in my office while Mr. Brase (they don't as a rule say Rev. or Pastor in Canada) is conducting services and I can hear every word he preaches. And I tell you, we should have more such preachers who preach the Gospel like Mr. Brase does; and as long as he preaches the Gospel like he does, and I am pastor here, he is welcome to use this church." How did I find out about this? Not to mention any names, suffice it to say, the source was most reliable.

The Canadian Thanksgiving Day is the second Monday in October. The day before Thanksgiving, namely on the Sunday before, we would have an all-day celebration with two worship services and a potluck dinner at noon. For this special celebration we would rent a hall the town owned which cost us five dollars. To make sure we could use the hall for our celebration on the designated Sunday, I had to go to the town hall a month or more in advance and make the arrangements by signing the "town book" and paying the rent in advance.

In the morning, we would celebrate a festival of Missions and in the afternoon, the festival of Thanksgiving. We would have one guest preacher for both services if we were able to get one. Preachers lived "far" apart in that big land. And few of them had less than five preaching stations. To serve as a guest preacher, the services in their own parish would have to be canceled. The home pastor had to be present to make sure the program for the day would be carried out as planned, especially in a young congregation.

These annual festival celebrations were inaugurated about four or five years after I began work in Lloydminster. The attendance was, comparatively speaking, good; and compared to Mission festival and Thanksgiving Day attendance in America today, it was excellent for a new-born congregation. But what is more, the people enjoyed the celebration and fellowship at the potluck dinner which always was bountiful and delicious. What is still more, however, is that the public was made conscious of the fact that there was a Lutheran congregation in town.

Two of these festivals I shall never forget. One is when we had the honor of having the president of Concordia College in Edmonton for our guest preacher. He is a good preacher and also a good musician. For the afternoon service our organist, or rather pianist, could not be present. So our guest preacher also served as pianist to lead the singing. And whereas most young congregations sing too "draggy" — also some old ones — and our guest preacher also being a choir director, he played the music as it should be played so that the hymns would be sung as they should be sung. It was the Thanksgiving service in the afternoon. He was almost half way through the second verse when the congregation came to the end of the first verse — almost that bad, anyway. But by the time the whole hymn was sung, which had more than four stanzas, the congregation was singing with the music and enjoyed it. They rejoiced in the Lord, singing their songs of gratitude unto Him.

Another such Thanksgiving festival I shall never forget. "As I remember it," my wife did not go to church with her family of girls that morning. She sent them off to church by themselves and then walked in the opposite direction which took her to the hospital. While there, a beautiful but strange little girl came about the middle of the afternoon to keep her company and to make her home with us. The doctor brought the good news by phone to the hall where we were celebrating the Thanksgiving festival and informed me that mother and daughter No. 5 were well and happy. That truly was something to be thankful for even though daughter No. 5 did not bring with her a five dollar raise in salary for her "proud" parents. But we welcomed and loved her just the same. Children are gifts of God. He has given us five, one of whom, as I wrote pages back, He has taken to Himself in glory.

We named our new daughter Lois Johannah Catherine. "Lois" for a Biblical name. "Johannah" in memory of her grandmother on her papa's side, and "Catherine" in memory of her grandmother on her mamma's side. Often she, therefore, signs her name as Lois "J.C." even though she did not add a "Penny" to our salary. We loved her in spite of that. She was so cute. And God also loved her in Jesus, the Savior, for through Baptism He washed her perfectly clean of all sin, both original and actual, and took her into His family of saints and made her an heir of heaven, which she is to this day because He has kept her in faith all these years and her parents pray that He keep her and all her sisters and their families in the true faith unto the end.

Daughter No. 5 did, however, increase the family allowance check the government gave every resident family in Canada for the children up to their sixteenth birthday. The check was issued to the mother and amounted to about thirty dollars a month.

As I already wrote, World War II, especially the first year or two, caused us Lutherans some difficulties. As soon as the war broke out, the Royal Canadian Mounted Police, during the night, rounded up a group of German people and hauled them off to some concentration camp. I had been conducting worship services in the German language in their community. I had a suspicion that they were "Hitlerites" because I happened to see some of their children greet each other with the "Heil Hitler" greeting. But that did not strike me as anything bad or unlawful at the time. They were merely children. I thought nothing of it until the fathers of some of these children were roused out of bed to take a midnight "moonlight ride" with the Mounties. I did, however, know that some, if not all, of these people were members of the "German Bund" which, in itself, was no crime. Then a light was turned on in my mind, and it was not "moonshine" either. But what an awkward position that placed me into, you can well imagine.

These people I served lived in the Hillmond area. One Sunday when I was there to conduct a German worship service, we had the service in the home of a family who had a fairly large house. There were more people there than usual. Some were strangers to me. This was the time I saw some of the children greeting each other with the "Heil Hitler" salute. While I was conducting the services, more people arrived. Some joined us in the worship service, mostly the women and children, but not all and very few of the men. When the service was drawing to a close, I could hear band instruments tuning in an adjoining room, which was rather disturbing. I could not stay long after the service because I had more services to conduct, but I was there long enough to learn that the large number of people were there more for a "German Bund" meeting than a divine worship service. Some of them came from quite a distance and most of them I did not see again for not too long after this World War II broke out and the Mounted Police took most of the men away to some concentration camps for the duration.

One day I found myself in the Mounted Police office or barracks as they called it. It was above the post office. I cannot recall now why I went there. Whether I was asked to come there or whether I had some other reason of my own to go and consult the Mounties, I do not remember anymore. But I know that I was there and, as I remember it, I was asked to give up my shotgun and to have my finger print taken. I argued the point and wanted to know why. He had asked me what descent I was. I told him that as far as I knew it was German, but it could be French because the name "Brase" had been seen in the newspaper written with a breve — Brasé.

The Mounty insisted that I have my fingerprints taken and turn in my gun. He took my fingerprints then and there. My gun I delivered later. I argued that I was a full-blooded American and that I, for a little relaxation and exercise, go hunting for various fowl several times a week during hunting season and that that was all I used my gun for. I believe I always used up all my shells, or made sure I did, by the end of the hunting season and, therefore, had no shells for my 12-gauge double barrel shotgun until I bought some again when the next hunting season opened. But the Mounty insisted. He said he was sorry but had to carry out his orders and they were to take the guns and fingerprints of all who were considered enemy aliens. Wow! When he said that I nearly blew my top and said one word loud enough with a question mark that there was no doubt he heard and understood what I said and meant. "ENEMY-alien?" it was.

Then I told him a few things. I said, "I am a 3rd generation American. Both of my parents were born in the United States. My father's father fought and was wounded in the Civil War. He was a Union soldier. And furthermore, I asked him, "what would have become of England, of which Canada is a part, if it had not been for America with its soldiers and wealth winning the First World War?" He did not argue the point but rather agreed and said he was sorry he had to do this but he must carry out orders from headquarters in Ottawa. Then he said, "I, too, like to go hunting the way you do and when I do, I will stop by and take you along." "A lot of good that will do me without a gun." I replied. "You will have one, when you are with me," he said. But he never did pick me up to go hunting with him. And why not? No, not because of what you, a reader of this, may think. He and his three deputies were very busy and just did not have the time.

At another time when I was in his office, he said he was sorry that he did not find time enough to go hunting and take me along. He took me into the room where they had stored all the guns they had collected. What a collection! It was a blessing for some people because some of the guns were falling apart and some were wired together with hay wire, like we used to keep our Model T Fords together and going. In spite of what he had to do, he was a very kind and friendly man and I did admire and respect him.

I was also to report to him every time I would go further than 75 miles from Lloydminster and where I was going. I had several preaching stations beyond 75 miles, especially when I served the St. Walburg parish north of the North Saskatchewan River and 60 miles beyond the end of the railroad. In that parish I would be 140 miles from home the way the crow would fly it. But I never did report.

The Mounty also told me to have my wife come to his office to have her fingerprints taken. She never did go. So one of his deputies came to the house and took her fingerprints. Sometime later he told me that that was the lowest thing he ever had to do and felt like crawling out underneath the door. She, too, had to report. She did it regularly, possibly to give me some secret protection. Quite sometime later when my wife did her regular reporting, he said to her: "Your husband definitely does not like or believe in reporting." She replied: "Can you blame him?" "No," he said. I still refused to report to the police every month as though I was a criminal on parole.

How many people knew about this, I don't know. Possibly very few, if any. The work of the church went on as always and we did not lose any members but slowly and steadily gained a few more. Our troubles on account of Canada being at war against those "awful" Germans, who are one of the most industrious people on earth, were not over. One evening after Bible Class, which was held in our residence, members of the Bible Class were accosted by a citizen and business man of our growing town who had a few too many wet spirits under his belt. As he was on his way home, wobbling or walking past our home and the people were just leaving (some of whom were of English descent), he made some remarks about these German Nazis (which are not printable) and wanted to know what they, the English people, were doing here in this Nazi meeting. One of our members, who is a little quick on the trigger, was just ready to land a blow. I quickly jumped in between and prevented the blow from landing, thank God. That would have been disastrous for us if it had landed. I spoke to the man and led him away a little and told him to go home. This incident was not to get out so I asked the people to go home and forget about it. The next morning I went up to the Mounty's office to report the incident. He had asked me to report to him if and when anything like that took place. The Mounty was irritated at what happened and wanted to know the name of the man. I refused to give it to him. I said that I did not want this incident in the records but merely reported incidents to him as he had requested so he might know what we were encountering and could decide whether we might need some police protection. "OK," he said, "off the record, I want to talk to the man and set him straight on how things are." This apparently he did for we had no more such incidents and no adverse publicity. He did, however, some time later, get some real good publicity in the whole country round about and that I shall write about next.

It was a year or a little longer after the outbreak of the war and it was time to make arrangements for the use of the hall for our day of festivities. I was very busy at the time so I asked a young man who had come to my house for something, but I do not remember what it was, to go and ask for the use of the hall. He was one of our church elders. I explained to him that all he had to do was tell the town clerk our plans and date, sign the book and pay the rent. I then gave him the five dollars. He came back shortly with a peculiar look on his face and told me that the town clerk told him that we would have to get permission from the chairman of the Properties Committee. That seemed odd to me, too. We never had to do anything like that before. This chairman was one of the butchers in town. So I sent the young man to the butcher shop to ask him for this permission. The man was not in the butcher shop. The elder came back and reported this to me. So I sent him to the man's house. He had one spirit too many under his belt and made remarks about us Lutherans that I can't spell or write. He was able to philosophize enough to say that we were Lutherans and Luther was a German. We were followers of Luther and therefore we were Nazis and Nazis could not use the hall for a meeting.

My elder came back with a worse look on his face. I then said that I would go and speak to him. Before the day was over, I did. But this time his wife came to the door. I told her who I was and what I came for. She said, "Why don't you go to the Mayor and ask him?" While she was advising me to consult the mayor, her husband shouted from somewhere in the house — probably the bathroom — some words I do not and don't want to remember. I then told his wife that I was on my way to the mayor. I went directly to the doctor's office because the doctor was the mayor and also our family doctor — a good doctor and a very fine man who respected the Lutheran Church. He had attended a Lutheran college somewhere for part of his training in medicine. There were still several patients in his office. So I waited. It was late afternoon when I was able to tell him about our problem. He listened carefully and then replied by asking. "Why did you not come to me in the first place?" I explained to him how we had always done it and never had any difficulty at all. He assured me that we would get to use the hall. He could not, however, just override his council member but would go and speak to the other council members and get their approval. I was to come back the next day. I did and I was informed that that man had gotten ahead of the mayor and had gotten the support of other council members.

The mayor again assured me that he would see to it that we would have the use of the hall on the Sunday before Thanksgiving. He then asked me to write a letter to the town council and also told me what I was to write. This I did. This was the beginning of a goodly amount of correspondence between the town council and me. The congregation did not know anything about this. I was fighting this battle alone. But time was running out. Would I win the battle in time for our festivities? Thank God we did. God is never too late with His help. Our festival went on as though nothing unusual had gone on before.

The town council, however, had demanded that I make a public statement either before one of our worship services or during the service or after the service. While all this correspondence went on, there was a town election and new council members as well as a new mayor were elected. So I was now dealing with a council that had a few new members on it. I had kept a copy of all the letters I had written and, of course, all their letters written to me. I then wrote one more letter which contained the following: 1. A statement of loyalty which the Walther League (our Synod's official young people's society at that time) had printed on the front cover of their District Paper at the outbreak of World War II. 2. Articles from our Lutheran confessions which stated what the duty of Christians is over-against the government. 3. Statements made by Luther on this subject. 4. My request that our Statement of Loyalty which they now had, plus all the correspondence which was carried on between the council and me be printed in the next issue of The Lloydminster Times, which was our weekly town paper at that time. This they did. And I am grateful to God for I firmly believe that He put that idea into my head to have all this made public. And what good publicity that was for our church and congregation! Everybody in all the country round about now knew about our Lutheran congregation in Lloydminster. We did not lose one soul but kept right on growing. All glory to God! "He works in a mysterious way His wonders to perform."

There was, "As I Remember It," another time I went to the police barracks but do not now remember for what purpose. But it served a good purpose. I was talking with one of the deputies when the sergeant stuck his head out of his inner office and with his finger motioned for me to come into his office. After I had entered, he closed the door and told me that I need not report to him, just to forget about it. Well, that is just what I had been doing and now I could do it legally.

At another time he told me that he could get a permit for me to get my gun back. He filled in a paper which I had to sign and I needed a witness. "Where should I get a witness?" I asked. "Here," he said, "I will be your witness." And he signed it and mailed it to Ottawa. Now all I needed to do was wait for the permit to arrive. I waited and waited and here one day it arrived, just one day before the war ended. I believe I still have that permit. So it goes, also in Canada, even to a preacher.

Several months after I, or we, had won our war with the town council, our troubles were not over, but also these turned out to be blessings in disguise. Jesus Christ is still the One and Only Head of the Church and always leads on paths that, no matter how rough and rugged, always lead to victory and greater blessings. But before I write about that "As I Remember It," I must write about another joy-instilling thing I experienced.

A day or two after our Statement of Loyalty and all correspondence between the town council and me appeared in the newspaper, which took up most of the back page of the newspaper, the town clerk, a thoroughbred Englishman direct from England, came to my house and expressed his sorrow over what happened, clasped my hand and congratulated and thanked me for the expression of loyalty and wished me success. From that day on, every time we met on the street, he would stop and chat a while. I know he was sincere and meant it. He had other good thoughts about me and it made me feel happy. I deeply appreciated his action and will never forget it. He was the only one of the town's officials to say anything complementary or otherwise.

This whole ordeal and trying experience was, of course, the fruit of hate against Germany and anything that, and everyone who, in any way, had any relation or connection with anything that appeared to have a semblance of being German. And the devil, of course, used this hateful attitude to try and hinder and, if possible, to land a fatal blow to the church of the true and saving Gospel. God, however, used this hatred and ordeal to strengthen and further His Kingdom in Lloydminster and thereby defeat the devil and his evil intentions. Yes, all glory to God who brought us, His church, safely through these trying times and continued to bless the preaching of His Word just as He promised: "My Word shall not return unto Me void, but it shall accomplish that which I please and it shall prosper in the things whereto I sent it" Isaiah 55:11. God makes *all* things work together for good to them that love Him, as it says in Romans 8:28.

In addition to the problems I had to cope with and serving my own parish of five or six preaching stations, I was once more saddled with the vacant St. Walburg parish which gave me twelve preaching stations to serve and took me as far as 140 miles one way from home. That was the distance as long as the North Saskatchewan River was not frozen over and the ferry could navigate. When I had to cross the river on a bridge, it was 260 miles one way.

There were children to be instructed and confirmed in the saving faith. How and when could I accomplish all that in such a far-flung parish? My wife got a good idea — a wife is supposed to come up with good ideas, right? Isn't that what a wife is for, conceiving good ideas? The idea born was this: Have all the children from both parishes come to Lloydminster for a month for instruction. Where to house them — that was still a problem. I spoke to the members of First Lutheran about it. One of our very loyal and faithful young couples, married only a short time before this, offered us their house. The young man was entering the military forces and his wife was going with him. Other people offered some beds to set up in their house, also a table or two for desks. So far so good! What about food?

The people of my own parish were in full agreement with the plan. The St. Walburg parish likewise accepted the idea and offered to help furnish some food. I set the date when the school was to begin. All kinds of food came with the children, except one sack of potatoes. The father had laid it on and/or fastened it to a fender but it slipped away and he had lost it.

The girls slept in the young couple's house about three or four blocks from our house. Classes were held there — also in the kitchen. My wife and our little girls slept with the girls. The boys and I all slept in our house. Everybody had to rise by the clock, eat by the clock, retire by the clock, go to class by the clock, study by the clock. Oh, we also had time set aside for play, and all did play. All meals were served in our house. My wife had made up a schedule and posted it. Every child's name was on it and what each one was to do each day: help with meals, prepare food for the meals, wash dishes, make beds, clean, etc. It all worked like a charm and everyone enjoyed doing it.

There were fifteen children in the class. They were confirmed as a class. That Sunday we really filled the Baptist Church edifice to capacity. This is an experience in my ministry in Canada I shall remember to my dying day and likewise the efficiency with which my helpmeet, whom God gave me, managed the board and room end of it.

Did all these children remain faithful? A pastor wonders. Will we all meet in heaven? I pray so. Possibly a year or a little longer after the ordeal with the town council (which was drifting further into the hidden recesses of our minds and the congregation was flourishing), we received a notice from the Baptist congregation that their church edifice would no longer be available to First Lutheran congregation. I am drawing a blank from my memory as to what their reason was for requesting us to seek other facilities. Nor do I remember for sure whether the Baptist congregation had a change in pastors sometime before this request was made of us. It does, however, seem to say somewhere back in my memory that there was a new pastor when the notice came and that he had plans to use the church in the afternoon for some program or whatever it was. Be that as it may, I do remember for sure that we did receive a notice to seek other facilities. Also this "blow" (if that is the right description of it all) turned into good for us. But when the notice came, I was shaken and quite at a loss as to just what to do.

It was in the winter when the notice came. The same day I received the notice — or was it the next day — I saw a member of the congregation who, I believe, was president of the congregation at the time, driving past our house in his bobsled. I ran out and stopped him and gave him the notice to read. After he had read it, he said: "Good, that is the best thing that could happen to us." His remark, as one might say, "floored" me. "What do you mean?" I asked. "Now we will just build our own church. I am glad. That is just what we will do," he said. And he drove on. It was cold and I was not dressed to be out in the cold. I did not have time to put on my overcoat. It takes a layman at times to set a pastor's sight straight. Yet I now had also this problem to think about and perhaps lose a wink or two of sleep.

We had no property of any kind in town, except an organ. We had an opportunity to buy a good used reed organ at a bargain and we bought it before we had a church of our own. But we talked about building a church around the organ some day. The Baptist congregation had only a piano in their church and they were kind enough to let us place our organ into their church. They likewise offered to keep the organ until we had a place for it.

A committee was chosen to look for a suitable lot or two. The most pressing need, however, was to find a place where we could conduct our worship services. The Baptist congregation did give us time to relocate. We did continue renting their place of worship for several more weeks, but our people were anxious to relocate after being requested to leave so that the Baptists could make full use of their church. We had also used their facilities for Sunday School.

The only place I could think of at the time where we might hold our services was the funeral parlor. When I suggested that possibility, my suggestion was met with decided opposition, especially on the part of a certain lady. She would not come to church there with dead people lying in the next room. Was she afraid that one might reach out through the wall with his boney hand and choke one of us? But there were also a few others who were not too keen on worshipping in a place like that. So we did not worship among the dead. The town hall, which we used for our festival services, was too large, and too cold in the winter. It was an old building. The building which housed the offices, the fire engines, etc., had a larger meeting room on the second floor. We got permission to use that for a while. In the meantime I was working on a "collapsible" pew. I succeeded, although it was not exactly collapsible. I made stools with a back on them from 1" x 4" boards. I sanded, stained, and varnished planks ten or twelve feet long — am not sure anymore of the length — and 1" x 12" boards the same length. The planks I laid on the stools and the boards, into which I had screwed an eyescrew, I hung on the back of the stools, into the edge of which I had driven a finishing nail. They worked and served the purpose well.

I should have had a patent on them. I would not now in my old age have to depend on Social Security.

We now conducted the services in our home, saving rent. Sunday morning I, with help from Mama or the daughters that were old enough to help Daddy, would set up the pews — six or eight; I am not sure anymore. After the service I would take them down again, line the stools along one of the walls in our front room, stack the planks and boards on them. They took up little room and could be used for seating. During the services we likewise used all our chairs. We had a five room house and often we would have people in every room with attendance ranging from 40 to 60 people. In the meantime, the committee acquired a corner lot on 48th Avenue and 48th Street, 2 blocks east of our house. Now the building fund had to be pushed.

We chose a building committee and busied ourselves with building plans. Without any trouble we got a building permit from the town of Lloydminster. We dug a basement 24' x 40', if I remember correctly. After we had that done, we were informed that we must get a building permit from the federal government also. This became another trying experience. We made the necessary application for the needed building permit. The reply from the federal government was slow in coming and when it did come, it was a refusal to issue a building permit for a new church edifice because all building materials must be conserved for essential purposes. You must remember, dear Reader, World War II was on. The war was in its second year and things were not fairing too well for the allies at the time. But the reason given: "Building materials must be conserved for ESSENTIAL purposes" struck me the wrong way and got under my skin. I made a reply in which I expressed my feeling on the "essential purposes" and attempted to show the writer of the refusal that the church is most essential to bring the war and any problem and difficulty the country is encountering to a successful conclusion. Furthermore, I emphasized that it is the church and its God-given mission that sustains and raises the morale of the people at home and those in the military forces. And I asked him where the morale of our people — in the military and out of the military — would be without the church, which through its chaplains, is marching right with the military forces. I likewise had explained why we had to build at this inappropriate time. The reply to my letter was a long time in arriving. When it finally arrived, we were still without a permit.

It was another refusal.

We decided to settle for a permit for a basement and use it for a place of worship. We waited for a reply. But my patience was wearing very thin. One day as I went to the post office — here was a reply? No, dear Reader, nothing. Just like the day before and the day before that and the day before that, etc., etc.

On my way home from the post office, I walked on the opposite side of the street, which I never did otherwise. Just why did I do so that day? I've often thought of that. I just don't know. All I can say is that God guided my steps in that direction. On the opposite side of the street a lawyer who had spied on us various times had his office. I walked by his office. I saw him sitting at his desk. That was enough for me. About three or four doors past his office I turned around to go see that lawyer. What possessed me? Why go to him? And for what? I did go and I thanked God for it for I am absolutely convinced that God was sending me to this man who spied on us but who, also, could help us. And he did.

Seated across the desk from the man. I told him what I had done about getting a building permit from the federal government and that I had "struck out." He said that he was not surprised. "I know the man," he said, "I used to practice law in Ottawa. My office was right across the street from this man's office. He never did see your letters. One of his deputies answered your letters and just made no exceptions. I will write the man who is the authority in that branch of the government, and I assure you that in two weeks you will have your permit." I thanked him and left "that man's" office happy and hopeful and grateful.

Two weeks and possibly a few days later the phone rang right after the close of the Sunday morning worship service held in our house. The congregation was still there. I was making announcements when the phone rang. I answered the phone. It was "that man." He said, "I have good news for you. I am phoning now because I imagine your congregation is still there and you can tell them that your permit should be there in a few days." That was good news. The permit arrived that week and I must say that "that man" had a change of heart and mind concerning us Lutherans, the followers of that great German man Luther. All glory to God, whose hands are never tied, who works in a mysterious way His wonders to perform, and who turns the evil and destruction the devil intends to bring upon God's kingdom into good and glorious victory. Praise the Lord!

During this time another unexpected thing happened. The town put our house on tax-sale. We were renting. We had paid the rent every month. What did the owner, who did not live in Lloydminster, do with the rent money? We could get nothing from him for repair or painting. The interior decorating or painting my wife and I did ourselves out of our pocketbook. But what to do now about a house? The officers of the congregation took this business in hand and they ended up buying the property. Now we owned an organ, a lot for a church, and a house on two lots. Who can or would say that the Lord God was not good to us and was not blessing First Lutheran Church?

Problems were, nevertheless, before us, but they always turned out to be blessings in disguise. Due to the delay of the permit from the government, our basement, or rather "hole in the ground," filled with snow in the winter, with water in the spring, and caved in. We pumped some of the water out but, due to the spring rains, it never did dry out.

After the wheat-seeding was completed, work began in earnest on the building of the basement. When the foundation was completed, for which we poured cement, work, of course, stopped for a while. In the meantime, we tried to get the basement dried out but never really succeeded because of the rains. And it seemed that water was seeping in from the bottom. Oh, how several of us worked dipping and pumping water out! We had borrowed a pump which we had to work by hand. We set it on the foundation and oh! I wish I knew how many hours I stood there pushing and pulling that pump handle back and forth, back and forth! And how many hours a few others did the same thing! It had to be done. He could not pour the floor as it was: wet, muddy, goo-ey! In the meantime, the sub-floor was laid. Now the "hole" at least was covered. But it would take longer to dry out. A roof was built over the basement.

Time marched on: Fall was approaching. We had some kind of a stove in the basement to help dry it. Finally the floor was poured. Then the inside was neatly finished and shortly before Christmas we dedicated our own place of worship to the honor and glory of God. We were happy and grateful.

The pews I had made were set up in our place of worship and if my thinker is functioning properly, I believe we made more such pews. If that is not true, then just what else we used for seating I cannot recall. I do remember that we built a platform about six or eight inches high all the way across the one end of the basement. We built a lectern which we set in front of the platform to the left side from the congregation's point of view. Our organ was at the other end of the platform. In the middle stood our altar. The altar was a large veneer dry goods box which I obtained as a gift from the dry goods store. The top of the box was possibly five or six feet by about three feet. I used one of my wife's white tablecloths for altar coverings. A wooden crucifix, which I had received as a gift, I placed on the altar. We also had two candles on the altar.

The walls and ceiling of the basement were finished with plaster board and painted. If I recall correctly, there were three windows on each side. We had a very neat and churchy looking "basement church" from the inside. But from the outside, some people had a different idea. I found out about it this way: To get the grounds in shape for a lawn, we planted potatoes. One day when my wife and I were weeding and hoeing, a young couple slowly drove by. They turned the corner to see more of our "basement church." They were really looking it over. They stopped, got out of their car, and walked toward us. They wanted to know what this building was. It was not painted on the outside nor did we have a church sign out front. We did not tell them but invited them to come in and see for themselves. They were truly surprised and made some very complimentary remarks about the interior but had a different idea about the outside. The young man said that they were struck by that kind of a building in town and wondered who would have a pig barn in town. They just had to see it. Well, they did. And the outside front end did get a coat of paint by one of the members whose son was to be married in the "basement church" soon. We also put a church sign on the front end. The only entrance was at the back.

The water problem in the basement was still with us, especially in the spring. Many a time a most faithful member whom I had instructed and confirmed several years before was at the "basement church" early on Sunday morning dipping and sweeping the water out. It did not cover the whole floor, of course. We inquired what we could put on the floor to seal it. A special sealer was recommended, of which we applied several coats. It helped. The floor would get moist occasionally yet, but eventually: No more water!

We had our own place of worship, the congregation grew and became stronger, and soon the room was well filled with people worshiping God.

During the time we were building our "basement church," we were offered some good lumber by a man who had a lumber mill up north a ways in the bush. Lumber was a little difficult to get during the war, especially good lumber. So we bought from this man at a good price but we had to haul it ourselves. This we did and then stacked it in piles on the sub-floor under the roof in such a manner that it would dry out and still remain straight.

The first vice-president of the Missouri Synod even honored us with his presence one Sunday and preached to us on the occasion. He had been at the Manitoba-Saskatchewan District Convention representing the president of our Synod. He was also to be at the Alberta-British Columbia District Convention which met the week after our convention. Lloydminster was on his way to Edmonton, where the convention was to be held. I took him with me to our home. That Sunday afternoon and evening I took him with me to two of my preaching stations which he seemed to enjoy very much. He made some truly complimentary remarks and also gave some good advice. Oh, yes, also during our problems and building program, I served all the other preaching stations regularly, including the St. Walburg parish. I had no problem keeping busy.

An experience well stuck in my memory is when a young couple knocked at my front door one Sunday noon shortly after coming home from church. They wanted to get married now, right now, and they were in a hurry to get somewhere yet that day. I asked. "Do you have a marriage license?" "No." the young man replied. "Well, you cannot get married without one and where and whether you can get one on Sunday, I don't know," I told them. "Where do you want to get married — in Saskatchewan or in Alberta?" I asked. "If in Saskatchewan, then you cannot get married today because there is a ten-day waiting period after application for a license has been made and both of you will have to have a blood test. If in Alberta — well, there you can get a license and get married all within an hour or less." "In Alberta," the young man said. So I phoned the issuer of marriage licenses on the Alberta side and explained to him the situation and asked whether he would issue a license on Sunday. He replied, "I will. Have the couple come to the office. I will be there in a short while."

That I might marry them, I had to do it in Alberta. Hence, I went to the office with them and also took my wife for we would have to have witnesses. I didn't know where we would find a second witness. So after the issuer had issued the young couple a license, I asked him where we might find another witness. He said, "I'll be a witness." I married them right there and then in the issuer's office and they were happily married and on their honeymoon within a half hour after they had applied for a marriage license and I had filled in and signed the marriage certificate. I do remember this marriage, but I do not remember whether I got "paid" for my services. Oh, well, whether I did or not, I am not any the richer nor poorer for it, but "as I remember it," they were happier after than before and I hope they still are.

During the war the federal government made an appeal that all able-bodied people who possibly could should help the farmers harvest the wheat crop. Due to the war there was a shortage of farm labor. Hence, being a good American living in Canada, I also helped. I worked for a young couple of the congregation at Artland. They had two small children. A year or two before this I had instructed and confirmed the lady of the family. He was our organist and also taught Sunday School.

My job was driving a steel-wheel tractor pulling the binder. There were very few, if any, combines at that time. In the morning while my "boss" did the chores and some "stooking" — to my American readers, it is "shocking"* — , I was given time and opportunity to do some sermonizing, and I also did some in the evening if I was not too tired.

Saturday afternoon I was allowed to go home to get ready for the Sunday services. But there is one Saturday I shall never forget, and that I ever did get home alive I owe alone to the gracious protection of the Lord. We had a big rain late Friday night and early Saturday morning. There were no graveled roads. The roads were muddy and traveling was difficult. I had to drive many miles in the lower gears to get through the mud holes and keep moving. After several hours of such driving — I had forty miles to go — the lower gears would constantly slip out. I do not remember what make of car I had but I do know it was one of my various second-hand cars that kept me broke.

It was getting dark and I was only about half way home. On a high

*A stook, also referred to as a shock or stack, is an arrangement of sheaves of cut grain-stalks placed so as to keep the grain-heads off the ground while still in the field and prior to collection for threshing. In shocking or stooking, the sheaves are leaned against each other so as to cover and protect the ears from the weather, and act as a roof to the shock or stook.

grade my car suddenly slipped back and forth and as I applied the brake, it headed for the ditch. I released the brake and stepped on the gas pedal to get down and through the ditch and the fence, which I tore down. I was in a pasture. I got out of the car, examined the lay of the land, and looked for a place where I could get back on the road. I found a place where I hoped I could get back on the road but I wondered how I would keep my car from going over the grade into the ditch on the other side. I had to take the chance and I prayed the Lord to help me. He did.

I got up onto the grade and managed to get straightened out and get my car to stay in the muddy track. Only a short distance and I was off the grade. I could drive with only one hand because with the other one I had to hold the gearshift to keep it in gear. It was near midnight. I was running low on gas. I came to a small town but there was no life in it and, if I remember correctly, no filling station either. I was getting very tired and like the gears on my car, worn out. After I was through the little town, I stopped along the roadside and slept.

When the sun was shining into my face, I awoke. I proceeded on my way home again. But what about gas? Well, I would have to depend on a farmer to help me out if the tank got dry. But would a farmer sell me any gas? During the war there was a purple gas which was for farm use only. It was unlawful to use it in a car. Well, fortunately I did not need any purple gas or any other color gas. The roads were getting drier and when I was eight miles from home, the dust was flying. I arrived home near 11:00 A.M. I was a dirty preacher from my experience of the night before and by the time I got cleaned up and to the church, I had no people there anymore to whom to preach. Whether I served the other preaching stations scheduled for that Sunday afternoon and evening, I do not remember. But I probably did.

While writing about the trip above "as I remember it," a drawer popped open in my memory which contains a story of another trip which also had to do with mud, but this time it was gumbo.

My wife and I and, I believe, one or two of our girls had taken a couple and their son to visit some friends or relatives, or for business purposes, to a place a hundred miles or a little further southeast from Lloydminster. On our way home the next day, we came through an area where it had rained in the morning. We had no difficulty until we came to a stretch of gumbo. While it is raining or the gumbo is still well soaked, it is not sticky nor difficult to navigate in, except that it is a little slippery. Oh, but when it is beginning to dry, it sticks and clings like "Elmer's Glue," goes round and round with the wheels, fills the fender wells, the wheels get bigger and bigger, and before long they will turn no more and you are stuck. This stretch of gumbo was possibly a quarter of a mile long. We had a very difficult time moving ahead even in a lower gear. Finally we could not move. The gumbo was packed solid in the fenders and around the tires and was pulling the brake cables so the wheels were locked. By now some of you readers will perhaps be saying: "What a tale and tall story he is relating . . . wonder if he expects us to believe it?" Well, I am telling the truth. And I hope I can convince you by the following: We were right close to a farm place. I walked there and asked the farmer for help. He got his horses ready to pull my car onto his place. The horses had a very hard time pulling my car and staying on their four feet because the rear wheels would not turn. They were just sliding. Once the horses got out of the gumbo and had good footing, they pulled the car out of the gumbo and as soon as the car was out of the gumbo, the wheel cut a groove through the mud under the fender and turned again.

Once we had the car on the man's place, we took the wheels off and dug four wheelbarrows of mud out of the fenders and from the wheels. The children had fun throwing mudballs at his buildings. When I looked up and saw what a mess they were making on his buildings, I had to stop them from having fun. Once we had the mud fairly well scraped off, it was nearly evening. If I remember correctly, we had supper with these people.

After that we made it home without any trouble. Just to what extent we remunerated them for their help and hospitality, I just do not remember. But in those days in a young country, there was much more helping one another without pay than there is today. People were more equals in those days and hospitality was a way of life for them.

Having finished my story about the trip south where we were stuck in the gumbo, another experience was unearthed in my memory. It has to do with rocks. I hope you will not mind going south with me once more to Alsask, the west end of the Rosetown parish I served immediately before being transferred to Lloydminster.

I was staying the weekend at the home of a family whose two sons I was instructing for confirmation. I did this every time I came here for services. The public school teacher had her room and board with this family. When I was instructing the boys in the first article, which speaks of creation and preservation, and told them what the Bible says about the creation of the world — that God, by the power of his Word, brought the world and all that is in it into being and upholds all things by the power of His Word, the boys told me what the teacher had told them, namely, an evolutionistic theory that the earth was once solid rock and that for millions of years it was crumbling and finally things began to grow, etc. And concerning the story of the Garden of Eden and Adam and Eve, she told the children that that was not true but was just a nice story the people of many years ago liked and wrote into the Bible. A first grade girl told her mother what the teacher had said. The mother told her daughter that she was to tell the teacher the first thing in the morning that what she had said about the beautiful Garden of Eden and Adam and Eve was not true but that the Bible is true, that it is God's Word, and that she was not to teach such things. When the teacher asked her who told her that the Bible is God's Word and is true, the child said that her mother told her and she is right.

After I was through with my class with the boys, I would visit for a while with the father of the boys over a cup of coffee and a snack. The teacher would join us. I used this opportunity to speak to her about her teaching the children evolution. She said that she had to teach what the textbook said. I told her she did not and then showed her how very foolish it was. I asked her whether she really thought the Canadian Pacific Railroad would build a railroad over the mountains or if anyone would have built the large beautiful hotel in the mountains at Banff if the rocks were constantly crumbling and they knew that someday the whole thing would tumble down. She answered: "Oh, I never thought of that." "And furthermore," I said, "this man here, our host, is a farmer and every spring he has to haul rocks off his land. He has done this for about forty years now. These rocks are brought up by frost and heat. He has piles of rocks that he has hauled off. Now, if, as you say, the earth was a solid rock and has been crumbling for millions of years, how come he has to haul rocks off his fields every spring? There should be no more rocks, don't you think so too?" Her answer: "I never thought of that." I then gave her a book on evolution which showed how utterly foolish it is, how unscientific, how wrong and contradictory. She read the book and when she returned it, thanked me and said, "I will never teach that stuff again."

One of the trips to Maidstone, forty miles east of Lloydminster, I will never forget. It was in spring. I went there to instruct an adult. It was evening. The highway was graveled. The snow was mostly all melted. Water was everywhere. The highway was reasonably good except for one big mud hole, a muskeg. The thing was almost bottomless. Next to the road was a big pond of water. On my way to Maidstone I made it through the muskeg. But on my way home about eleven o'clock, it was a different story for several reasons. I knew where the "danger" place was, namely, shortly after a slight bend in the road because of the railroad. If I did not make the bend, I would be on a trail taking me to the wrong side of the track. I was watching for this bend. But shortly before I got to it, it snowed a shower of big flakes which looked like dinner plates coming at me. (Big snowflakes is one thing Texas cannot brag about.) They stuck to the windshield. I had to try to keep my windshield clean with a wiper operated by hand. I was driving a "Model T" again. When I slowed down, the lights would get dim. I could not see enough to see the road clearly. The next thing I knew, I was on the railroad crossing. I backed up and managed to get on the right road. Only a short ways to the "sump-hole" now. Every once in a while I would drive in low to have brighter lights. The snow had stopped. When I saw the hole — about ten or twelve feet long or wide, whichever you please — I stopped, let the motor run, and got out to investigate. The tracks were deeper than they were when I came. There were a few ridges left by trucks that had churned through. Now if I can stay on those, I may make it. If not: stuck in a muskeg. My car would rest on the ridges and my wheels would be free. I did not stay on the ridges; hence, I was stuck. I walked around in a field to try to find a stone or post or something to put under the wheels. Nothing. I tried to jack up the Model T to dig the mud out from under the body but the jack went down instead of lifting the car. So I pulled the jack out of the mud and it was quite a pull. Then with a branch from a tree next to the road or with a tire tool, I tried to dig the mud away from under the car. It was a hopeless job: What to do?

It was now near midnight. I decided to sit in the car and hope for someone to come along the highway. But everybody was wiser than I was. It was getting colder by the minute. What I and my clothes looked like, you can well imagine: wet and muddy. I was getting cold. I started the motor to get a little warmer and more comfortable. I got sleepy. I stopped the motor and tried to sleep but before long I was cold again. I got out of the car, drained the radiator — there was no anti-freeze then, at least I had none. It was possibly three A.M. by now. There was a town about a mile or two down the road. I decided to walk and go to the depot where it would be warm. But the train not being due for an hour or more, the depot was still locked. So I went to the hotel and sat down on a chair near the door. How good that felt! There was no one awake there. I fell asleep in the chair. When the train arrived, several people came to the hotel but went right up the stairs and to bed. They had something I did not have: a reservation. But I had something they did not have: wet and muddy clothes. I went back to sleep until the sun was shining brightly into my face and woke me.

I stationed myself at a window to watch for some living human being to show up. It was probably eight o'clock or a little later. I kept watch. I saw no one. Canadians seem not to get up early if not necessary. But if one had known about my plight, I am sure that one would have been up to help me. I decided to walk the streets. I tried the "Chink's" place. That is a cafe. Still locked. I came to the livery barn, entered it. Oh, how cozy warm: Why did I not go here in the first place? And there was a nice pile of hay, or a pile of nice hay, where I could have stretched out my weary self and had a really good, undisturbed sleep. Well, what could have been did me no good now. I went back to the "Chink's." Still locked. I went back to the hotel. Everybody still in slumberland. It was getting near nine o'clock. Oh, there is someone who went into the post office. He came out and went right back home. Before long another does the same. Another one. He goes on to the corner, turns right. I go after him. He is an implement dealer and has a small garage. That's my man! After a few persuasive words and the promise to pay him, he and I were on a tractor with a chain and a pail for water out of the pond for my, no, the Model T's radiator, and we were headed for the muskeg. After a little while my Model T was out. The good man on the tractor unhooked the chain and was on his way back into town. I broke the ice on the pond, dipped out some water with the pail, filled the radiator, started my reliable Model T, and was on my way to return the pail and to pay the man. I did. Then I headed for the cafe and you might know why: it was almost ten o'clock. Still locked! Must be a "night" club. So I headed my Model T in the direction of Lloydminster and forty minutes later had a good breakfast and lunch in one, which Mama prepared for me. It made me feel good all over. What a mama and good cook God gave me. That is how the good Lord took care of me. I was safely back home and well taken care of. "Praise the Lord, O my soul, and forget not all His benefits!"

While serving also the vacant St. Walburg parish, I decided to try to get the whole parish together for a "one day convention." The purpose was to inform these people about Synod and its world-wide work, how Synod works, why a synod, and to try to get them to widen their horizon so they would have a world-wide outlook on the church and its work and not only think of themselves when thinking and speaking of the church. Christ directs our eyes to the whole world when He says: "Go ye into all the world and preach the gospel to every creature."

Seldom, if ever, did any of these people attend a church convention and possibly heard little, if anything, about plans and decisions made at a convention. So I laid my plans and put them before the various congregations and preaching places in the parish for their consideration and acceptance or rejection. Well, we did hold a "one day parish convention." I did the same thing in my own, the Lloydminster parish.

It meant a lot of hard work on my part: prepare a special sermon, prepare for the various matters pertaining to Synod — missions, finances, etc. — which I chose to present, and also give the people an opportunity to ask questions and discuss matters. No resolutions were to be made. In the morning I conducted a worship service. Whether I also, after the service, presented some Synodical matter, I no longer recall. At noon we had a potluck dinner. After some time for visiting, the convention proper was called to order. We carried on for possibly three hours during which time I spoke almost continually. I can well remember that my voice got weak and once was gone completely. When I could no longer make myself be heard, the people could ask questions. I had a member come up on the stage — we held the convention in a hall because we had no church building where the convention could be held — and I would let that member answer the questions, or I whispered the answer to him and he would give the answer.

It was hard work, but enjoyable. How else could these people learn to know more about the Synod and its work, which was their work? "Synod" is a Greek word which means "a going together of many on one way." From comments made by various people, I know that it was enjoyed, was profitable, and worth the work put into it, for I also know that God lays His blessings upon the work done for Him and His kingdom.

After these conventions, I had trouble with my voice every once in a while. I finally visited a throat specialist. He made a thorough examination but said that organically there was nothing wrong with my throat or vocal chords. He then asked whether I smoked. I did smoke at that time. He asked what I smoked. I said, "mostly cigarettes unless I am home. Then I smoke my pipe more. But I am away from home possibly more than I am home." Then he wanted to know what kind of cigarettes I smoked, whether tailor-made or whether I rolled my own. "Both kinds," I said, "but possibly more that I roll myself." I did that because that was much cheaper and I had a little machine to roll them in, and my older girls could even do that for me. Not to smoke at all would have been still cheaper. Why didn't I quit? Foolish man! Maybe I could have bought a new car then and not only second-hand cars. These and the cigarettes must have kept me poor.

But back to the doctor who said that tobacco does not harm your throat but it is the paper that does the damage. "If you must smoke," he said, "smoke a pipe." Who must smoke, except he who is not man enough to throw off the filthy habit?! I was not. I was a slave until May 2, 1962, when I had my second heart attack. Then I was in Wisner, Nebraska, pastor of St. Paul's Lutheran Church. If one of the readers of this book is a smoker and is hereby convinced it would be better to quit the bad, health-destroying habit and does quit, I would be amply rewarded for writing this. Is it worse for a preacher to have a bad habit than for a layman?

As I remember it, I was scheduled to perform a marriage at one of my preaching stations about fifty miles from Lloydminster that almost did not take place. No, not because the bride or the groom felt it was a mistake and therefore backed out or did not show up. Yet, the groom did not show up at the hour the marriage was set for. What could the matter be? He was not at home, nor at the church, but somewhere between these two places in the mud. Oh, it had rained and, if I remember correctly, for several days. He had about sixty miles to come. His brother, as I remember it, was responsible for his deliverance, not from but to the marriage. And his brother was using my car, of all things, to deliver the groom. Because of the rain and roads, I had taken the mixed train the day before, I believe. I wanted to be sure of being there on time. The bride's father met me at the train. So there we were — a bride, one witness, a preacher, but no groom, and one witness missing. A witness missing was no worry. They are cheaper by the dozen and we could have nicked anyone out of a dozen. But that would not work for a groom and probably is not advisable. We waited patiently. Every once in a while we went outside to see if we could see a groom on the horizon. It was dreary, wet, and muddy outside. No groom on the horizon. After a short while — "whiles" which seemed like hours — we did the same thing. Finally it paid off. "Here comes" not the bride, but "the groom," we could now sing. "Please make for him room." And that also brought the missing witness. As the saying goes: "The show must go on," so also the wedding. And it did. In the fear and name of the Triune God they were joined together in holy wedlock and pronounced husband and wife.

What the groom and witness looked like when they arrived in the mud in the preacher's car, I let to your imagination. Whether they had their "Sunday-go-to-meetin'" clothes with them to change into after arrival, I just do not remember, but I imagine they did. What do you, who is reading this, think?

Of the various marriages I performed, there are a few that seem to have fixed themselves permanently in my memory. There was the one I performed at Battleford. It was not so much the ceremony, but the celebration of the wedding that was somewhat unusual. It consisted of two parts. The first part took place at the home of the groom's parents who were Scandinavians. Here we had a delicious wedding dinner with all the trimmings, Scandinavian style. After this was completed, we moved to the home of the bride's parents who were Ukrainians. The ceremony, by the way, was held in the afternoon. It was early evening when we arrived at the home of the bride's parents. Here we enjoyed another delicious dinner served Ukrainian style. Was it really possible to enjoy two dinners with only a few hours between the two? Well, dear Reader, "seeing is believing." We did enjoy it. (But I must inject here: as I am writing this in 1975 I can't help thinking of the thousands of hungry and starving people in the world today. May God have mercy on them and move us, who are still living in abundance and luxury, to do as the Lord Jesus said to His disciples and to us: "Give ye them to eat." Matthew 14:16. And as He multiplied the meager supply then, He can also do this today so that no one goes to bed hungry. But are we doing as He asks us to do? Is it so difficult to understand why we are reaping inflation and shortages and other great problems? Failing to believe and do according to God's Word never brings a blessing.)

Excuse me for being carried away by a situation in the world of 1975 that really disturbs me. Now let's get back to the Ukrainian style wedding celebration back in the 1940's. In the course of the evening there was some singing and dancing. As the celebration progressed, the young couple was stationed behind a table and the Ukrainian people, especially the older women, sang in their language. I, of course, did not understand a word. But from what happened I have an idea what the words they were singing meant and were asking the people to do. This is what the people, a few at a time, did: they walked up to the table, congratulated the young couple, gave a gift of money, and then, as I remember it, the men — most of them — received a kiss from the bride and the women received a kiss from the groom. Then the best man and maid of honor gave the donor a glass of wine, who, after drinking most of it, poured the rest of it over his or her right shoulder. Why? I don't know.

When there were no more "donors" approaching, there was a little more dancing. Then the Ukrainian women, mostly older women, began singing again and before long a few more people approached the table and the same procedure, described above, took place.

I was sitting at a good vantage point where I could observe just what was happening. Next to me sat a young Englishman who was a good friend of the groom. He approached the table, did as the others had done, but did not get a kiss from the bride. When he returned to his chair. I asked him: "How come?" He did not know. I asked him: "What did you give them?" "A half a dollar," he said. "Now watch," I said, "I am going to wish them well, make a donation, and I am going to get a kiss." I did. I also did the same with the wine — a little bit of it. (Oh, the floor was a mess by now!) When I returned to my chair, I said to the Englishman in a jesting manner: "What did you expect for fifty cents?" What did I give? Well, Reader, will it satisfy you to say: more than the Englishman gave? But I enjoyed the celebration. It was different. It was like they do it in their homeland in the Ukraine, USSR. Here in Canada they were free to do as they pleased as long as they remained within the law.

This Ukrainian bride regularly attended my church services with her husband and desired to become a member of our Lutheran church. During the time of instruction she really applied herself, by far more memorizing than I required of her, especially Bible passages. She would write them out on a sheet of paper, attach it to a cupboard door or someplace where she could see it while cooking or washing dishes. One day when I came to her home and saw the paper hanging over the sink or stove — somewhere, I do not recall just where — I took it down and made a remark or two about what the Bible verses taught and she would recite them almost perfectly. What a joy to instruct a person who is so anxious and interested to learn the saving Word of God. She came from a Greek Orthodox home. Her husband was one of the brothers I was instructing several years before this when I fell asleep while instructing, which I already wrote about pages back. She and her husband are still loyal to and active in the Lutheran church.

Our services in the Battleford preaching station were still being conducted in the country in the homes of the members. We were anxious to conduct our services in the little town of Battleford. I did some canvassing there and also scouted around for a place of worship. There was a small vacant church building at the southwest edge of town. I cannot recall who or what denomination owned it. But we did get permission to use it. It needed a good cleaning and some repair. We did what we could to make it usable. There were no pews in it but, as I remember it, some benches without backs. No altar nor pulpit, if I remember correctly. My memory seems to tell me we built a lectern and used a small table one of the members donated for an altar, covered it with a white cloth, and for every service altar flowers were furnished by some member. The members pitched in with the hope of making it a successful venture. The young couple, whose wedding celebration I wrote about above, was especially enthused and exhibited their enthusiasm. We did have a few visitors out of Battleford at most of the services but most of them had other church connections or were not interested, only curious. Our undertaking just did not succeed, mostly because I was still, or again, serving the St. Walburg parish as vacancy pastor and just could not do justice to the work. You know, Reader, what happens when you have too many irons in the fire: one or two turn out to be a fizzle, right?

Well, well, the Board of Missions finally gave me a vicar. He was to serve particularly in the St. Walburg parish. I took him to the parish to acquaint him with the lay of the parish as well as with some of the people, especially the leaders in the various congregations and preaching stations.

Now I should have more time to concentrate on my own parish. But the Lord had something else in mind for me. The latter part of the summer I usually arranged for mission festivals at several places, especially in the larger and more active preaching stations or congregations. I had such a festival arranged for Battleford. We would have two services — forenoon and afternoon — out in a grove somewhere. Up here, as I already wrote, we were in the Park Belt area where we did have all kinds of bluffs. At noon we would have a potluck dinner — or lunch, if you wish, but what a lunch! Then we would visit for a while and then have another worship service, centered on the Mission of the Church. After this we played a few games and races with the children and also a softball game for all who would take part in the game. There was no sex or age discrimination! Then we went home to rest and relax, but the farmers to do their chores. These were really wonderful and much enjoyed festivals.

I can recall another such festival out in the open at Artland. We had a guest speaker for the afternoon service. When he arrived he informed us that World War II had started. We had a goodly number of German people in the Artland congregation and they seemed to accept that tragedy rather calmly.

Before we had our own place of worship in Lloydminster, we conducted our Christian Education services for several years on a bluff just outside of Lloydminster, followed by a potluck dinner and a Sunday School picnic.

Now back to the Mission Festival I had arranged at Battleford, but which was never held. As I wrote above, the Lord had something else in store for me. My plan was to go there on Saturday to help get things ready. Our two older girls were going with me. Early Saturday morning I awoke because of a pain in my chest. I finally woke my wife and asked her to prepare a mustard plaster for my chest because it felt as if I was getting a bad chest cold. I had to preach two times the next day. The obedient and obliging wife she is, she did it at once. After some time I believe I fell asleep for a while.

The time was here to get up and get going. But the pain in my chest was so severe at times that I could not stand up straight. But I had breakfast and walked uptown to do a little business before I could leave for Battleford. Walking uptown, I had to stop occasionally because of pain. When I returned home, I got ready and the two girls and I left for Battleford, nearly one hundred miles east. Every once in a while I nearly doubled up because of the pain. Graciously the good Lord brought us to our destination which was the home of the couple whose marriage and celebration I wrote about, but it was now a few years later. They persuaded me to go see their doctor in Battleford, which, thank God, I finally did.

It was now the latter part of Saturday afternoon. I was the last patient for the day in his office. He questioned and examined me thoroughly. I could see by his expressions that he did not like what he believed he found was my trouble. Finally he told me that he was sure I had a coronary occlusion. "But," he said, "to be sure, I would like for you to go and have another doctor examine you. Go to Dr. 'So and So'; his office is — no, you cannot go there. His office is on the second floor and you must not climb stairs. You go directly to the hospital and I will have him examine you there." I told him what plans I had for the next day, Sunday. He said that they must be canceled. I also told him I had a car here and must do some phoning and notify my wife. He told me I could leave my car in the parking lot at the hospital.

After I left the doctor's office on my way to the hospital, located in North Battleford across the North Saskatchewan River, I first stopped at the central (telephone) office in Battleford. Uh, oh, the central office was on the second floor of the building. Now what?! I decided to climb the stairway slowly. I made it. I did my phoning.

I am racking my brains to try to recall how our girls got back home and likewise my car. But I just do not recall. All I can say is that all three did get back to Lloydminster and I did get to the hospital where I was put to bed in a hallway because of the crowded condition in the hospital at that time. When the doctor came about an hour later and found me parked out in the hallway, he raised a "rumpus." The nurses hurriedly moved patients around and soon I was in a four-bed ward which had, I believe, six in it. I was instructed not to get up or exert myself in any way for anything but to ring for a nurse for anything I wanted or needed.

The light of day had gone and the darkness of the night had come. Likewise the doctor had come again and brought the other doctor with him who then examined me and voiced the same opinion the first doctor had voiced. Medication was prescribed and the nurses were given orders and I was ordered to relax and rest, which I did, or at least tried to do. My main thoughts, of course, were of my family as well as the people who were to celebrate a Mission Festival the next day. Yes, my whole parish and the vacant parish were in my mind, trusting God that He would provide them with the preaching of the saving Word and keep them in His love and grace. As far as I and my condition were concerned, I committed all into the hands of our almighty, loving God, who doeth all things well and promised never to leave us nor forsake us. And He says: "Call upon Me in the day of trouble, I will deliver thee, and thou shalt glorify Me."

The doctor came twice a day the first few days. As I began to feel better, he came once a day. About the third or fourth day I said to the doctor: "I would like for you to tell me exactly what happened and what my condition is. I was honest with you and told you exactly how I felt and I ask you to be honest with me." With a hand on each side of me, he leaned over me, looked straight into my eyes, and said: "Mr. Brase, you are really only half alive. You had a very bad coronary occlusion. But if you follow orders precisely, it can and will heal again." I thanked him for his frank report and promised him that I would follow orders. And I did, trusting God to bring it to pass and heal me.

I was in the hospital ten or twelve days when my wife managed to come to see me. The doctor told me that I could go home providing I would have someone to take me home in a car in which I could lie down on the back seat and have a place about half way home where I could stay for several hours to lie down and sleep.

I had a member about forty miles from home whose wife I had instructed and confirmed only shortly before this. They gladly took me in and gave me a bed to lie down on and while I slept soundly for an hour or more, they also entertained my wife and our driver. After a little lunch we continued on our journey homeward and under God's protection, we arrived there safely.

The doctor at Battleford had already phoned our family doctor in Lloydminster and informed him as to my illness and condition. Before very long our family doctor made a call on me, examined my heart, gave me strict orders, likewise my wife. I was to have no visitors of any kind; not even were my girls allowed to come into my bedroom — only my wife to give me the attention I needed. I was not allowed to read anything, not even the headlines in the newspaper. Just lie in bed and look at the ceiling! After a month or longer, I had a mental picture of the ceiling in my mind with every soot and little speck in the right place. How differently heart conditions are treated in 1975!

It was probably harder on the younger girls, Cordelia and Lois, not being allowed to come in and romp around a little on my bed, than it was on me. But they did visit occasionally at the open door. My wife regularly and faithfully came in with an ice pack which she was to lay on my chest over my heart several times a day, likewise give me a pill every so often, and then also a sedative at certain times, and, of course, also feed me, or at least "bring on the food." Without a complaint, she loyally and faithfully waited on me for several months before I was allowed to get out of bed and eventually walk into the kitchen to join my faithful family at mealtime. Before this, however, I was allowed to read some. It was fifteen weeks from the day of my attack until I again got the green light from the doctor that I could go back to work, with the instruction to take it easy at first.

I recall that before I had this attack, I was so worn out and tired that I nearly fell asleep driving and several times caught myself heading for the ditch which scared me and woke me for a while. Before long I was sleepy again and I would stop on the side of the road or off the road and take a nap.

The vicar had taken care of the St. Walburg parish and some of mine occasionally. First Lutheran of Lloydminster had a pastor from Saskatoon come to conduct services occasionally and they also held "reading services."

About six weeks before I got the green light to get going again, a family of the Lloydminster congregation had a baby boy they wanted baptized and they wanted their own pastor to do it. They said they would come to the house and I should ask the doctor whether he would allow me to do that. He did and I baptized the boy and gladdened the hearts of the parents. God received the boy into His family of saints. When the doctor at Battleford learned from the couple who sent me to him that I was in the harness again, he asked them to tell me that he would like to see me sometime soon. I did go to his office and had an interesting conversation with him. I asked him: "Just what is a coronary occlusion and what causes it?" He had learned how much I was doing or trying to do. So he said: "Work has never hurt anyone, but when one does more than he is able and drives and pushes himself to get it done, it will eventually hurt him. That is what you have now experienced. From now on, don't overdo it and you can live a long time yet. An occlusion is like a blowout of a tire.

You get it repaired, you can and do use it again, but you know it has a weak spot, so you do not pump it up quite as much and you do not drive it quite as hard. That way it will last a long time yet. So will you if you do as I said. Then, also, I want you to keep your weight at 140 pounds or somewhat under." I was over by about 15 pounds at the time. He gave me a diet, mostly raw vegetables, which I really enjoyed, and my weight came down, down, but I never hungered to get my weight down. I was also to take a short nap every afternoon and I did, when it was possible, and I still do. Next to God's grace and goodness, that is the reason why I can write about it twenty-eight years later.

One more thing: when I was permitted to have visitors, but still stay in bed, the mounted policeman who took my gun from me, took my fingerprints, wanted me to report to him, but who, nevertheless, was a gracious and a perfect gentleman, came to visit me, which I most deeply appreciated. I remember part of our conversation was on income tax. I told him I had never filed but with my salary and five children, I was sure I would not have to pay any income tax. He advised me not to file until the government asked me to. Yes, Canada also had such a "thing," but I never did file because the government never asked me to file. But it did continue sending the monthly family allowance checks, a certain amount for each child according to the age of the child up to sixteen years of age. Our monthly check amounted to thirty-some dollars at the time.

And another incident nearly was forgotten and I just can't understand how that could slip out of my mind. I am sure you can't either. If you, lying on a bed, were put into a hearse for a ride to a mental hospital, you probably would never forget that ride. I can assure you that it is some experience which really gives a person a creepy feeling. I know, because I had such a ride. That was the day after I was admitted to the mental hospital in North Battleford. Now what do you, dear Reader, imagine I was taken to the mental hospital for? Were the doctors trying to find out whether I was really "all there" or perhaps had lost a "marble"? No, Friend! The only electro-cardiogram in North Battleford was at the mental hospital. The doctors wanted to read my heart and its actions. That done, I was taken back to the hospital in the same way. So I have had two rides in a hearse already. Before I was dismissed from the hospital, I was taken to the mental hospital again in the very same manner for the very same purpose. Four rides in a hearse already! Who else can boast that? And I have one more ride coming unless Christ, the Lord and righteous Judge returns for the final judgment before I get that final ride in a hearse. In that case, I, together with you and all the other believers in Christ who will still be alive when Christ returns, will meet the Lord, our beautiful Savior, in the air, and enter with all risen believers of all ages and peoples and nations into the eternal glories of heaven to live there forever with Him with whom there is fulness of joy and pleasures forevermore. May this divine truth of God remove all fear you may have for that final ride in a hearse and fill you instead with a desire, as Paul the apostle expresses it, to depart and be with Christ, which is far better. Philippians 1:23. This is most certainly true.

World War II had come to an end. My gun was returned to me. Now I could do a little hunting again in the fall and I did, especially when I was in the Battleford area where I shot bush grouse. As the day was coming to an end, the grouse would fly up to roost high in the trees. As I walked on the bluff, they would stretch their necks to see what was moving down there on the ground. I finally was able to "take their head right off." What a shot! I must brag a little. Everybody does that once in a lifetime. The bush grouse had a lot of breast, the meat of which is white and very tasty.

When the war had ended, the Communists in Russia became very active and persecuted the Christians especially, and any others who did not agree with them and did not submit to them. Many tried to escape to make their home in a free land like Canada and America. Some succeeded; others did not. One family from Latvia succeeded, except for one son. If I remember correctly, he was sick at the time of flight. A faithful friend had him in his barn where he covered him with hay and took care of him otherwise. The Communists were suspicious. They came and searched his place, stuck a pitchfork in the hay here and there, came close but did not strike the boy. "O give thanks unto the Lord, for He is good." The other members of the family separated into small groups and agreed to meet in a certain village in western Germany by a certain date. By the grace of God and under His protection they finally arrived in Canada, came to Lloydminster where they had relatives in our congregation. In their bodies one could see what they had endured to become free, but in their faces one could see the joy for the freedom that God helped them find and they sang with rejoicing, expressing their gatitude to God.

One of their favorite hymns was, "Holy God, We Praise Thy Name," Hymn 250 in The Lutheran Hymnal. Although we were conducting all our services now in the English language, they readily consented to sing that hymn in church. That was something they could not do for some years under the Communists. We did have a goodly number of members who could still understand the German tongue. By this time, however, our congregation was truly cosmopolitan, consisting of at least ten different nationalities. But they all enjoyed the singing of this Latvian family, for they harmonized beautifully. It was only a short while that they were with us. They had to find work and a new home which they looked for and found in British Columbia. The son they had to leave behind recovered and then also succeeded in escaping and eventually came to Canada.

Vacation Bible School is something I very much wanted to conduct, especially in First Lutheran at Lloydminster. But whereas we lacked the necessary rooms, I asked the public school board whether they would permit me to use the school closest to our church. After I explaining at length what I would do and promising to leave the building in good and presentable condition, the board granted permission. So we had a Vacation Bible School. But my memory does not seem to have recorded how many pupils, nor how many teachers, nor how many children from outside our congregation we had. But we had enough for several rooms and I do remember the children enjoyed it, likewise the teachers and I; and it was another opportunity to sow the seed, which is the word of God, and that is all He wants us to do. He gives the increase and His promise is: "Thy Word shall not return unto Me void" but bring forth fruit. Only eternity will reveal how much fruit the seed of His word brought forth. So let's keep on sowing the seed — the results are in God's hands.

A Sunday evening Bible class, which I called "Doctrinal Information Period," or something like that — I may have had the name "Lutheran" in it also, I don't recall anymore — was also held. The purpose of it was to draw people not Lutheran or who were unchurched. I advertised the "class" in our only newspaper in town at that time: "The Lloydminster Times," a weekly, sometimes also a little "weakly." I gave the subject to be presented and discussed a prominent place in the advertisement. I followed the three articles of the Christian faith as presented in Luther's Small Catechism. Attendance at these lectures or presentations was from fair to good. But when we got into the second article and I had advertised that the doctrine of the divinity of Jesus Christ and His Saviorship would be presented for discussion, our attendance really swelled, and mostly by people not of the Lutheran or Christian faith.

When I entered our basement church that evening, I was most pleasantly surprised to see about a dozen strangers or visitors there already. My head swelled a little and I possibly said to myself. "Boy, you're really good and going over big!" But before the evening came to an end, my head had probably shrunk a little. As I emphasized that Jesus Christ is the Son of God, true God, very God of very God, these strangers began disputing my presentation. It didn't take me long to realize I had a group of Jehovah's Witnesses present.

They possibly had a definite reason for being present because I always tackle them on this doctrine which they strongly deny when their "disciples" make their house to house calls. I had had such a call from a woman quite some time before this and I knew they had my "number." This woman came to our house on a Sunday afternoon about one o'clock. At that time we were still renting the Baptist edifice and the services were in the afternoon. I was just dressing for church. As I went to the door I was trying desperately to get my shirttail into my pants before opening the door. Whether I succeeded, I do not remember. But as soon as I had the door open, she began reciting her memory work. Before she got to the third line. I knew she was of the Jehovah's Witnesses. Among other things, she said that these ministers in the various churches are not telling the people the truth. She was correct in some respects, but I said to her: "You come here and call me a liar and do not know what I tell the people." "No, I did not call you a liar," she said. "You certainly did," I said and walked toward her as I continued saying in no uncertain terms, "You see, I am one of those ministers you just accused of standing before the people and telling them lies. I am just dressing to go to church to conduct a worship service and, as you say, tell the people a bunch of lies." As I walked toward her, looked her straight in the face, my words backed her right off the porch and she hurried away saying, "I did not call you a liar."

A few months after that, maybe five or six, this same woman had a "run-in" with two brothers who were faithful members of our congregation and well versed in the Scriptures. They told her plenty and also that they were members of the Lutheran church which is conducting services in the Baptist edifice Sunday afternoons. "Oh," she said, "that Lutheran minister certainly is a firm man and sticks to his guns. I was there some time ago." As I said before, this may have been a reason they came to this particular presentation on the divinity of Jesus Christ to try to convince me that I was not telling the people the truth; or they were there just to give me a hard time like I gave one of their female disciples.

When they disputed my statement that Jesus Christ is the true Son of God, that He is "God manifest in the flesh," I directed them to 1 John 5:20 which states in clear, simple words that Jesus is "*the* true God and eternal life." They had Bibles with them; one of them even had a Greek New Testament with the translation into English between the lines. Well, I asked the one who did most of the disputing whether he would be kind enough to read that Bible verse — 1 John 5:20. After he had read it, I directed him to the verses immediately preceding verse 20 and asked him whom it is John is writing about. He answered correctly that he is writing about Jesus Christ. Then I again directed him to verse 20 and asked him to read it again. He did. Then I said, "there it clearly says 'He', namely, Jesus Christ, is *the* true God and eternal Life." Then the man with the Greek interlinear New Testament said, "Yes, Jesus is 'a' god. There are many gods. The devil also is one of many gods." But I said, "The Greek, in which the New Testament was originally written — in popular Greek — has the definite article which is 'the,' not the indefinite article 'a'." He said "The Greek does not have a definite article." I then asked him whether he had a Greek New Testament. Yes, he had a Greek New Testament. I asked him whether he could read Greek. "No," he said. Well, I then proceeded to explain what the definite and indefinite article in the Greek language look like. How did he try to get out of this one? He simply said that that verse, 1 John 5:20, was originally not in the Bible but that someone added it later on. "Well, well," I said, "if that is your argument and belief, then you can disprove anything you do not agree with, although it really is not a proof that it is not true. If you follow such procedure, I find no further sense or use in discussing this vital article of the Christian faith." I had also directed them to Isaiah 9:6 where the prophet, by inspiration of God, writes that the name of the Child that is born and the Son that is given should be called, among other names, "The Mighty God."

They, as all Jehovah's witnesses, also denied this truth and thereby rejected Jesus Christ and, therefore, are outside of the pale of Christianity and have no salvation because they have no Savior. Jesus Christ, true God and Man, is the Savior, and God tells us in Acts 4:12: "There is salvation in none other, for there is no other name under heaven given among men whereby we must be saved." Let us pray for these people that they come to the Light, who is Jesus the Son of God and only Savior, and also bear witness to the truth in their presence.

The Jehovah's witnesses, by the way, were outlawed in Canada during the war because they were considered anti-government. They were considered that because they put government into the same class with the churches regarding telling people the truth and misleading them. They absolutely refused to salute the flag and to give their allegiance to the country they lived in and which they expected to protect them. So they distributed their anti-Christian literature during the night sometime, dropping it in the front yards of the residents.

Another special opportunity to bear witness to the saving truth was given when the public elementary school set aside an hour every Tuesday afternoon for Bible storytelling. The pastors of the other denominations, of course, also made use of this opportunity. What they taught the children I do not know. We were assigned a definite room. As I remember it, I had the fifth and sixth graders.

I started with Genesis, chapter one, which gave opportunity to combat evolution. As the year progressed, I followed a book of Bible history. As I remember it, I used Egermeier's Bible Story Book, one of the best available and one that has been used for many years in many Lutheran families and the children love it. Try it and see!

This opportunity given by the public school was lost to us after a few years because it was abused, if I remember correctly, by some; one teaching doctrine instead of just telling the Bible stories as they are recorded in the Bible. In an opportunity like this, there must be no denominationalism. Just tell what God has to say in His Word and silently pray that He would bless the seed cast abroad.

One thing that troubled me some is the fact that most of our people, not only in my parish but generally everywhere, gave little or no thought to our institutions of mercy, such as our schools for the deaf, retarded, blind, and others that depended on the charity of us Christians. So I somewhere ran across the idea of indoctrinating my people to follow a crop-and-wage-sharing plan. A special envelope would be issued on which a list of charities was listed including also Missions and also a blank line on which the donor could designate what his or her gift was for. The donors also could check any of the charities or missions listed and so divide their gift among several.

When I had my plan worked out, I presented it to the various congregations and preaching stations, including the vacant St. Walburg parish which I was still serving. They agreed to my plan, some readily, others somewhat reluctantly. I, of course, explained to them that no one was obligated but their conscience, love, and willingness would have to be their guide. The plan for this special gift to the Lord was that farmers should give one acre of their wheat crop, no expenses deducted, and others should give as many days' wages that would equal one acre of wheat. The plan was pleasingly successful and was carried on for a number of years. The young couple whose wedding celebration I wrote about continued to do this for several years after I had accepted a call to the States. For several years we corresponded by letter and he wrote that the Lord gave His blessing for they were progressing very well financially. When I left there, this couple was far from being rich materially, but they were rich spiritually. How long they continued following this plan of giving a special gift to God as a thanksgiving offering for the gifts God gave, I do not know. I do know they are quite well to do and have really increased in property.

Yes, the plan was intended to be a special thankoffering to the Lord, something like giving God the firstfruits as He required of His people in the Old Testament. So the plan did have a Biblical basis and we in the New Testament have by far better reasons to bring special thankofferings to the Lord because we live in the time of fulfillment. God did send His Son to be our Savior. Jesus, the Son of God, did redeem us from all sin, from death and the power of the devil. We know that He gained salvation eternal for us in heaven because He ascended again into heaven to prepare a place for us. We know that we will some day be there because He will come again to take us home so that we can be with Him where He is in eternal glory. He gives us all this by grace through faith without any works on our part. "O give thanks unto the Lord, for HE IS GOOD, and His mercy endureth forever."

An experience I had one Sunday morning right after the close of the worship service in our basement church is still very much alive in my memory for I was suddenly and unexpectedly put on the spot by a total stranger who had entered our church after the services had begun. In other words, he was a little late. He wholeheartedly joined in the singing of the hymns, in the liturgy, and everything else. He sat on a chair at the very back of the church. I observed him and decided he was a Lutheran and was well acquainted with the order of worship. He listened well to my sermon.

The service ended and after I made an announcement or two, this man jumped up and walked toward the front, saying: "Pastor, may I address your congregation?" I was on a spot. What should I say? I no doubt had my mouth open but whether I said anything, I do not recall. I doubt I did. He did not give me a chance. He blurted out, "I am a Lutheran and I bring you greetings from Dr. Walter Maier, the Lutheran Hour speaker. I was with him only a day or two ago and talked with him and told him that I was coming here to drill an oil well for the Lutheran Hour. My brother and I organized and established a foundation or endowment in favor of the Lutheran Hour." He kept right on talking and could he quote and apply the Scriptures, and he really "moved" some of our members for I saw a few tears trickling down on even some men's cheeks.

This man was a real asset to our young congregation while there in Lloydminster. He was a very gifted man not only spiritually, but also mechanically, which he proved when he helped in the building of the superstructure of our church. My wife and I took the man to our home for dinner. While waiting for the dinner to be set on the table, he sat down at our piano, which he really could play. He could also talk well, which he did at the table and was so engrossed in his story that he dished over half of the bowl of vegetables on his plate. When he came to a pause and realized what he had done, he politely asked whether he could put some of them back. But he likewise was a good eater. As the meal was being drawn out, I became rather uneasy because I had two of my preaching places to serve that Sunday, one forty miles away and the other nearly another sixty miles further. I finally excused myself and left.

The one thing this man commented very favorably on a number of times was the Bible storytelling period I had especially for the children in church and, as a result, had more children in church than otherwise. I told the Bible story in place of one of the two Scripture readings, one year in place of the Epistle lesson and the next year in place of the Gospel lesson. I still think that this is an excellent idea and it does bring more children to church which is more than an excellent idea of man. It is God's will that also children go to church. "Of such is the kingdom of God" means the kingdom belongs also to them. And also the "old" children of God enjoy hearing the familiar Bible stories, are benefited by them, strengthened in faith, and are drawn closer to God. Can and do the Bible stories ever grow old and lose their power?

Writing about children brings to memory opening our home to a few and taking them into our family of girls to give them a home, at least for a while until they could be on their own. The first one we took in was a nine-year-old girl whose father had been killed by a horse and whose mother was confined to a sanitarium. She finally became a nurse, is married, and lives in Northwest British Columbia with her husband and her two girls.

The second one was a year or two younger than the first one we took into our family. She also had a brother who was taken into the family of one of our farmer-members. The father was divorced from his wife and had custody of these two children. How many the wife had in her custody I do not remember. The father was a shiftless, no-good character. The three were living in a shack of some kind in an alley. One of our girls did some "babysitting" for them. Our daughter got them to come to Sunday School. Then the boy was taken out to the farm of one of our members and the girl we took in. Where the father was at the time I do not recall now. Today both children are on their own. Where the boy is, I do not know; nor do we have the address of the girl. But we know she also lives somewhere in British Columbia, has a family, and is happy. She returned to Lloydminster for a visit several years ago and while there called on our daughter. This is how we know she is married, has a family, and is happy.

The first girl we kept we have visited several times in her home. On our first visit up there I baptized her two girls and regularly send them Sunday School lessons — have now for about eight or nine years. There was no Lutheran church in the town or area at that time. The older of the two girls was to enter school in the fall of the year I baptized them.

(Note: This last part about our visit up there and baptizing the two girls who adopted us as their grandparents — they have no other grandparents living — is not a part of my ministry in Canada "As I Remember It."

This happened after we were in the States.)

It has been snowing all day today as I write about my ministry in Canada "As I Remember It" and it reminds me of several trips I made in the winter the last few years we were in Canada and what difficulties I had in that white fluffy stuff, which is not very fluffy when it is blown into drifts. Then it is white hard stuff.

But before I write about these, I must write about getting stuck in the Battle River, which happened several years before my difficulties in the snow. Then I will let you, dear Reader, decide which is better or worse: to be stuck in a river or in a snowdrift.

It was a beautiful day in summer. I was at Battleford staying with one of our families for the night — the family whose son married the Ukrainian girl and whose wedding celebration I wrote about pages back. Well, as I remember it, I intended to visit a family on the other side of the Battle River. The good people I was staying with for the night wanted to save me from driving many miles to cross the river on a bridge. They took me to a place not very far from their home where people drove through the river. It was a wide, flat riverbed there with only one or two deeper holes which could be avoided rather easily. They carefully explained to me just where to drive. Well, here I went. Just before getting to the bank on the other side, I had to turn my wheels a little to the right or left. I don't remember which now. But I do remember that I did not turn them far enough and I slipped down into the hole, quite a hole. The car was resting on the front axle and engine. Stuck in the Battle River!

One of the boys went back to their home and came back with two big horses and chain or heavy rope. I don't remember which. Where was I? Where do you suppose? In the car in the river! But not for long anymore. Once they had everything ready for the pull by the horses, I and the car, after several really hard tries by the horses — and they had to pull hard and they did for the one front wheel had to come straight up — were out of the river. After we were out of the river, water ran out of the exhaust pipe. After examining the crankcase. I discovered there was water in that as well. So after letting the motor drip for a while and changing oil, I was on my way again.

At another time, also near Battleford, but in winter and when my wife was with me, we upset in the snow. We were on our way home on the graveled highway No. 5. The road had been plowed open but the snow was only pushed to the side of the road, not all the way off into the ditch. As we were coming around a bend, an "S" curve, a truck was coming around the bend from the other direction. We could not see the truck and the driver possibly could not see our car. But the real problem was that he was coming around the bend too fast and was halfway over on our side of the road. I turned out as far as possible, a little too far, to avoid a collision, for the snow pushed to the side of the road grabbed the right front wheel, pulled the car over toward the ditch, and very gently and slowly the car turned over on its side. I had a shovel in the back seat which landed on the window but did not break it. Nothing was broken, but the oil and antifreeze and the battery water drained out. The truck never stopped. He probably did not see us turn over. Now what? Well, first crawl out of the car. This done, we looked for a farm place close by. We started walking down the highway. We came to a farm place. My wife went there while I stayed in the cold on the road to hail anyone coming our way. No one came and nobody was home at the farm place. Finally a truck came along. He stopped but had no rope, no chain, or anything to help us. But he knew of a Frenchman about a mile around the bend who probably would be able to help us. He offered to take us there. We got into the cab and thus got to a place where my wife could at least be in a warm house.

The farmyard was quite large. I saw a man with a wheelbarrow hauling some meat to his hogs. He was cutting up a dead horse. I told the man my troubles. He said, "There is a team of horses in the barn. Help yourself." Then he went on pushing his wheelbarrow with the horse meat in it to his hog barn. I went to the barn. There were two large horses there and, fortunately, they were harnessed. But how would these horses of a French Catholic take to a Lutheran preacher? While my heart was beating like a trip-hammer as I walked between them. I did manage to get them out. I coupled them together. (I guess that is what you call it.) I then drove them to the bobsled. Oh, I had hooked up horses before! I worked on a farm during summer to earn some spending money and money for postage so I could send letters to my girlfriend while I was at college. And in those days there were no tractors, at least not very many.

The first thing needed was a neck-yoke. But I could not find it. I looked in the bobsled. Not there. Now what? I will have to ask the Frenchman for one. But what will I do with the horses while I go to where he is to ask him? I looked at the horses. They looked sleepy to me. I decided to let them stand there. I did. I walked over to the Frenchman and asked him about a neck-yoke. He said: "There is one there somewhere. Look for it." What a great help he was! I went back to the horses and began looking and scratching in the snow. Finally I found it, but not exactly near the bobsled. Before long I had the horses, hitched to the bobsled and drove over to where the Frenchman was. He was not quite ready to go yet. He walked to a shed and told me to drive over there. He came out after some time with a rope and a scoop, threw them on the sled, climbed in and took the lines and we were on our way to our car sleeping on its right side in the ditch. It was a simple thing to get it back on all four wheels. While the Frenchman stayed in the sled, I tied the rope to the handle of the right back door, but first I had to dig the snow away. Then I tied it to the sled which the Frenchman had backed up to the car. All set to go! The car was soon on its four wheels again. I untied the ropes. While the Frenchman got his sled around to the front of the car, I tried to start the car. But I did not succeed.

I now tied the rope to the front end of the car. In a short while the Frenchman had it back on the road heading for his place. As he was pulling the car, I put it in gear to try to start it. Nothing doing! Oh, there were no automatic gearshifts in those days. A motor could be started by putting the car in gear.

When we arrived at the Frenchman's place, he untied the rope and drove on. I had asked him for some wrenches so I could take the gas line off to find out whether it was frozen. He said, "There are some in the shed. Help yourself." After some hunting I found one. I used it and my pliers. The gas line was not frozen but my fingers nearly were, especially with gasoline on them. It was getting dark. I had quite a time getting the gas line connected again. I could not see well enough.

The car was parked right in front of the house. The light from the house would have helped if I would not always have to get in the way when trying to get the gas line connected again. Patience and perseverance finally paid off. Another hindrance was that my fingers were so cold I could hardly hold anything with them. I returned the wrench to the shed. Now what?

I went into the house to get warm. My wife had been there all the while. No hot drink was offered to either one of us. I now called a garage in Battleford about eight miles away. They were busy, he said, but would be out to pull us in as soon as he could get away. We waited, waited, an hour or longer. The men had come in for supper. The table was set, the food stood at the back of the stove, but no move was made to set it on the table. By this time I could have, in spite of all lack of hospitality, enjoyed even some French cooking.

I once more phoned the garage. He was still busy but would be out soon. About a half hour or longer — it certainly seemed much longer, he did come. As soon as we were leaving, the food was put on the table. Oh, yes, the Frenchman charged me for pulling my car out of the ditch to his place, but I do not remember how much. Whatever it was, it was too much. Since that day I steer clear of Frenchmen.

Once we were in the garage in Battleford, I felt much better. While the mechanic worked on my car, my wife and I headed for a restaurant — don't remember whether it was a "Chink" but probably was and probably was the only one in the small town of Battleford. Then, having something warm under the belt again — I doubt, however, my wife wore a belt — I must say, we both felt more comfortable and so made our way back to the garage. How long we waited for our car to be ready to go and take us home, I do not remember, but it certainly seemed a long time. Finally we were on our way — maybe about ten o'clock — and once more our loving, gracious Father in heaven brought us safely back home. We suffered nothing but a few inconveniences and unfriendliness. Whoever it was that took care of our girls did a superb job, for all was well on the western front. Lloydminster is about one hundred miles west of Battleford.

First Lutheran congregation in Lloydminster was slowly but steadily growing inwardly as well as outwardly. Our building committee, chosen shortly after we had completed our basement church, held many meetings, consulted other congregations who had recently built a church edifice, consulted an architect, drew plans, and likewise approached the Manitoba-Saskatchewan District with the request for a loan. During all this time, the building fund was being pushed and was growing. The committee had approached every member for a pledge as well as for a donation. The District rule was that a borrowing congregation must have a certain percent of the estimated cost of the church edifice in their treasury before it could get a loan from the District. We were able to satisfy the District.

But in the course of time, we would also have to get the necessary furniture, such as an altar, a pulpit, and pews. We had no idea what these would cost us. When we began looking into this matter, we were well aware of the fact that we would have to approach the District once more for an additional loan. That, of course, is normal, and the District wasn't too surprised. I have never heard of any building project — church, commercial, home, or what have you — that did not cost more than the original cost stated. Our request for an additional loan — I don't remember how much we asked for — was presented by me in person. It was the annual meeting of the District Board and all Counselors ("Visitors" at that time) were also required to be present. I was one of them. Again I must say it was the guidance of the good Lord that it was at this meeting our request for more money was made. There was one particular member of the Board who was decidedly opposed to our request, whose argument against an additional loan I had to "out-argue" some which way. I did. Had I not been present, I am sure we would have been denied an additional loan. When the final vote was taken, it was in our favor, for which we were grateful.

We needed a carpenter who knew what to do and who was capable of handling the workers. We had such in our congregation but none would accept the responsibility. Carpenters, good ones, were hard to find after the war. All were very busy. There were all kinds of men running around with a hammer and saw, wearing a carpenter's apron. We finally hired one of them.

The first thing we did was enlarge the basement another fifteen or twenty feet. My built-in computer, it seems, failed to record how much. When pouring the foundation, it became evident already what kind of a carpenter we had hired. If it had not been for one of the members who really understood carpentry work, the first wall that was being poured would have caved in — into the basement. He had repeatedly told the carpenter that it needed more bracing. The carpenter said it didn't. Finally this member, with a few other members, worked feverishly to put in more braces when he noticed the wall was beginning to cave in on them. They managed to hold it and even to push it back some. But it does have a little bow in it.

These were busy days and more were ahead, also for the preacher because he also walked around with a hammer (no saw or apron) and put in every hour he could spare to drive in nails, just like a boy who likes to drive in nails. Oh, I also did some sawing and I can still hear the boss saying to me. "Leave the mark! Leave the mark!" He did not say anything about sawing straight. He probably thought something when he picked up the board to use it.

I believe every male member helped whenever possible, also the man who came to Lloydminster to drill an oil well for the Lutheran Hour, who addressed the congregation the first time he attended our services, who emptied over half of the vegetables on his plate while talking. He helped whenever he could find time and opportunity to do so.

The extended foundation now in, the roof was taken off the basement church which we continued to use for our church services. The frame work was also done in a short time. The building began to take shape, including the castle tower on the corner to the right of the front entrance. The cornerstone laying ceremony took place when the basement was built.

Two of our members who were employed in town, sometimes three, and the preacher worked on the construction of the church nearly every night of the week for three to five hours a night. But at times the preacher was not at home because he had to serve the other preaching stations, instruct confirmands, do other church work, and also prepare his sermons.

Our attendance at church at this time had risen to an average of 90 to 100 per Sunday. Fortunately I was not saddled with the St. Walburg parish at the time we were building our church. One instance while helping build the church I just cannot forget. I was really scared and when I think of it, my legs still seem to get stiff. One of the faithful members, who worked at the church at night, and I were up high on a scaffold nailing 4' x 8' sheets of plywood we used for sheeting on the tower. The scaffold was not exactly level nor too firm and there was a breeze which caught the sheets when we lifted them in place. My member was as cool and relaxed as though he were standing on firm mother earth. I don't know whether he knew how scared I was even though I tried to act brave. Firm mother earth was a long step down there. But we completed our undertaking without a mishap. As long as we do not tempt the Lord but carry out our work or duty His promise applies: "He will give His angels charge over thee to keep thee in all thy ways."

Construction work on the new church edifice began after wheat seeding was completed. If my memory serves me correctly, time was taken off by most of our men, if not by all, for doing their summer fallow work. Then when it was time to harvest the wheat and other grains, work slowed down considerably. By that time the building was closed in and most of it was now inside finishing work. By this time we had fired the carpenter because he made too many mistakes. His mistakes cost us nearly two hundred dollars.

When we were putting the rafters in place, we ran out of space on the one side. On the one side of the building there was no place for the rafter. The carpenter had measured and marked the place where a hole had to be cut into the sheeting for the rafters to rest in. I helped saw the boards out where the rafters were to fit "into." The rafters had been put together down on the ground and then lifted into place. When we came to the north end of the building, there was no space for the one end of the rafter on the east side of the building. I happened to be the one who helped place the last rafter and all I could do was: just stay up there and hold it in my hand. Now what? Had I to become a permanent fixture up there to hold that end of the rafter? The rafters, of course, were "kitty-corner."

Before we began placing the rafters, after the places for them were cut, there was quite an argument between the carpenter and the man who had come to Lloydminster to drill an oil well for the Lutheran Hour. He knew what would happen and why. The carpenter had made his mistake at the tower where he began measuring. But he just would not listen to the advice given him. He insisted that he was correct. He measured it over several times beginning at the tower and always came out the same way because he started with a mistake at the tower. So he gave orders to get the rafters placed. The result I have already written about. The carpenter could not understand it. Finally he had to give in and let the "oil man" show him his mistake. Then he measured again beginning at the right place. We cut new holes, patched the first ones, and everything came out just right.

The two, carpenter and "oil man," had had several arguments prior to this over mistakes the carpenter had made. One day shortly after the "rafter mistake," the carpenter told the chairman of the building committee to keep that man (the "oil man") away from there or he would quit. There had been a few more "run-ins." The chairman of the building committee came to me asking me to settle the matter. I did and the "oil man" was wise enough and understanding enough not to come as often. He advised that we fire the carpenter. We should have let him quit when he said he would. That was a mistake we made which the following incidents clearly prove.

It was time that we think of pews. To determine how many pews we would need, I went there early evening one day when nobody was there and did some measuring. I discovered that the distance from the first window on the west side to the wall on the north end of the building was not the same as on the east side from the first window to the north wall. But why not? I just could not find the reason for it. I measured it over and over and always came out the same. By this time two of the members living in town arrived to work. I asked them to measure it. They came up with the same results. Two of the windows on one side were not directly across from the two on the other side. Pews on one side of the aisle should form straight rows with the pews on the other side of the aisle. So if the pew on the right side of the aisle is under the window, directly in the middle of the window, the pew on the left side of the aisle would be off center. And how would that look? But I did determine how many pews we needed but I don't, now in 1975, remember how many. I then wrote to a church furniture factory for a catalog and information, also regarding altars and pulpits. When we had decided what we wanted, we put in our order.

The next morning after the discovery I had made about the windows, I again was the first one at the church. I wanted to have the carpenter's helper, who was always there before the carpenter, do some measuring. He did and came up with the same results. I asked him to draw the carpenter's attention to it. He did. The carpenter did some measuring. He scratched his head. Can't be! He measured again from one end of the church to the other. Neither the south wall nor the north wall was crooked. He measured between the windows, stood there, and looked at them. He gave orders to his helper to tear out the two by six on the one side, saw the sheeting off so many inches, then put in a two by six, and fill in the other side of the window with as many two by sixes as needed — and to have it done before the others arrived. If I remember correctly, he had to move openings for two windows. Whether his helper had finished the job before any other members came to work on the construction of the church, I also do not remember. There are two things I do know for sure about all this: 1. That is the strongest part of the whole building, and 2. Those are the most expensive window "holes." In that part of the church there are five or six two by sixes nailed together.

This mistake was followed in short order by another, or it may already have been made but not yet discovered. This mistake was in the tower. Three crosses built of glass blocks were to be set into the tower so that they would also show up at night by hanging colored lights coinciding with the liturgical colors of the church year. One day while the carpenter was working up there cutting out the openings for the glass blocks, I went up there. "As I remember it," he was working on the third one. Was I disgusted when I saw them! They weren't in the right place and they were too low down. It even spoiled the looks of the tower as far as I was concerned. I told him that he cut the openings too low on the tower. He did not think so and tried to defend his mistake. But it was too late. Nothing could be done now to alter and improve it.

I went down and told a few of the members, above all the chairman of the building committee. If I remember correctly, a few others had found some unsatisfactory work. The next morning, before I got there, a decision was made to fire the carpenter. And who did the chairman say was to inform the carpenter? "Oh, no," I said, "that is not my responsibility, although I am much in favor of your decision. There is only one man who has that pleasant responsibility and that is the chairman of the building committee. Nobody else." "As I remember it," everybody agreed with me except the chairman of the building committee. He finally went to the carpenter up in the tower and did his duty — and did a good job. The carpenter packed up his tools, and possibly his troubles too, in his old toolbox and went his way. Oh, yes, he received his wages.

Now we had another "nut" to crack. It proved not to be a really hard nut. One of our members, a very capable carpenter although that was not his business, after much persuasion, accepted and had the promise of another capable man to assist him in the undertaking. From here on everything proceeded very nicely and no more mistakes, except one, if it can be called a mistake. I would say the men that did it meant well but our good carpenter did not agree with what they had done and did not accept it. It was a small job they did up in the balcony. They were instructed to finish installing the wallboard in the one corner which was not done. When they had completed it, they came to the head carpenter to report that it was done. "Good," he said and assigned them another job. A day or two later the head carpenter was up in the balcony to inspect whether all was completed up there. All of a sudden he called out with a loud voice, "Who did this patchwork here in the corner?" The men who did it confessed. Our head carpenter said, "Come right up here and tear it out and put in a whole piece. How does that look?! We are building a church, not a pig barn." It was done as ordered.

It was December already and we wanted the church completed and dedicated before Christmas. The last two weeks before dedication that church was like a beehive — men, women, young people all working. There was not a single drone among them, neither a married one. We accomplished it. The only thing missing was the pews. Dedication took place on Sunday, December 18, 1949, attended by 358 worshippers. The basement church was dedicated December 23, 1945. All glory and thanks to God, to whose glory and service we dedicated our House of God, for blessing our undertaking with success.

During the time we were building our church, the District made plans to have every congregation within the District visited and appealed to for gifts and/or loans for the Church Extension Fund. The solicitor who called on our congregation "crawled" around and between the scaffolding in the church and came up with a little over two thousand dollars. That was good and I was happy and grateful for this. Lending to the Church Extension Fund is very good and smart business. It serves two purposes: 1. It helps other congregations in their building programs; and 2. It helps the lender by earning interest. Yes, a loan to the Church Extension Fund works for the Lord as well as for the lender. It builds God's kingdom while it also builds the lender's little earthly kingdom.

Now that our building project was history, more attention could again be given to other matters pertaining to the church in my parish of now only four stations. First Lutheran was coming into its own, we had possibly a hundred or a few more communicants by this time, if I recall correctly. Through adult instruction in the chief parts of Christian Doctrine, the membership was slowly but steadily growing. Also, Lutheran families from other areas were moving into our booming town which was reaching city proportions.

Possibly it would interest my readers to know just how a missionary-pastor puts in his time in a multiple parish. Following is a summary of one year's activities. It is not a special year, but one just like any of the others. I took one of the small pocket diaries Concordia Publishing House in St. Louis, Missouri, given annually to every pastor in Synod. I took one out of the box I keep them in and it is for the year 1945. Well, that is my fifteenth anniversary year. I did not think of that until I wrote "1945." I did not even think of that while I made a summary of my activities in 1945. I also had the vacant St. Walburg parish to serve the last three months of 1945.

Here, now, is a summary of my activities during the year 1945: I conducted 132 divine worship services; taught Sunday School at least 70 times and confirmation class 91 times; baptized 14; confirmed 7; united 2 couples in marriage; conducted 2 funerals; made 86 calls (mission, pastoral, sick calls); held 58 office interviews; presented topics 12 times to the Ladies Aid; taught Bible stories in public school in Lloydminster; participated in 15 meetings, conferences, conventions; conducted Bible Class with young people; held choir practice with an adult choir and also with a children's choir; and in my spare time I renewed my acquaintance with my family and took them fishing once at Loon Lake. These activities put at least another ten thousand miles on my secondhand car which still kept me broke, but not for much longer.

A Big Decision was made by my wife and me to get a new car. We would try to borrow the necessary money and pay back a certain amount each month which would be just as easy to do as to constantly pay the garage for repairs and yet never be sure whether the repaired secondhand car would get me to the place I was going and then also back home again. And after we had the new car paid for, we would still have a better car than the secondhand cars we had had. Also, we would have a better "trade-in" on a new car. This Big Decision was made in 1950.

The next item on the docket was to find some good person who would trust a preacher and lend him some money. We had no intention of going to a bank. There was a Scandinavian couple who retired from a farm living only two or three houses from the church. He was the carpenter's helper during the building of the church. This couple attended our church regularly but were not members as yet. They and we were good friends. We would try them. Without any if's or but's, he was willing to lend us the money. How fortunate we were and how good God was to us. When I asked him to make out a note, he said, "That is not necessary." But I insisted on it. So he did but did not stipulate how much interest I was to pay. He insisted on "no interest." We agreed on a certain amount to be paid each month. This I did without fail.

I had already been to a dealer and knew the cost of the car I wanted and how much I would save if I drove it away from the factory in Oshawa, Ontario. So I made a deal, traded in my secondhand car, and had a new car out on order to be picked up at the factory. Several weeks went by before I received notice from the dealer that my NEW car would be ready on a certain date. I do not remember the exact date but I do remember it was early fall in 1950.

My wife and I were getting ready for a long bus ride to Oshawa, Ontario, to take delivery of a new Chevy right off the assembly line. Ain't that somet'n! We had no worries about our girls, several of whom were teenagers, and a few of the good members living in town kept a watchful eye over them, as did our loving Lord.

Several days of a rough ride on a bus brought us to our destination. We hoped very much that our new Chevy would give us a smoother ride back home. While there, we took advantage of a guided tour through the factory. It is amazing how quickly a car you see only pieces of at the beginning of the line comes out at the end of the line all in one piece ready to go. But as you go along the constantly moving line with men standing in one place, one doing this, another that, but always and only the same thing, and you see them cast their eyes on the tourists and hear them whistle at the girls, one really has to wonder if they did their job well and whether the car is going to stay together very long. I was hoping there were no tourists when my car was being manufactured.

I can now also understand why some of the screw holes, especially in the body, do not all line up and why some screws are put in crooked and why some are missing altogether. When one comes toward the end of the line, suddenly four wheels with tires on them come rolling down out of the ceiling (at least it looks that way) and one, two, three, they are fastened. The line is on the move. Now from somewhere above a body descends and in short order is fastened in place. All the various colors; but for the wheels, body and everything matches. It is truly marvelous what man has accomplished! what great and marvelous gifts with which God has endowed man! No wonder the Psalmist exclaims: "I praise Thee because I am fearfully and wonderfully made; marvelous are Thy works, and that my soul knoweth right well" Psalm 139:1.

With the body and everything else on and in place and fastened, the car rolls off the line. One man fills the radiator, another the gas tank, another jumps into the car, starts it, and, as the saying goes, like a bat out of purgatory, or faster, he drives the car out of the door in front of him. About twenty feet out of the door is a cement wall. It looks as though he is going to crash right into it. But he slams on the brakes, makes a turn to the right, and away he zooms to the parking lot or storage room. At least he is gone. And there is another car almost ready to leave the assembly line. One is a blue Chevy, another is a two-toned Buick, another is a red Pontiac. Everything is perfectly timed and matched. It was most interesting and instructive to see all this.

We were now ready to pick up our NEW Chevy. How would that feel? How would we, especially I, act? I guess we kept quite normal and after a few instructions as to the speed we may drive for the first five hundred miles, when to take out the break-in oil, how often to change oil, what grade or weight oil to use, etc., etc., we were on our way. But before we headed for home we made several visits. First of all we visited that faithful Dutch family who left Lloydminster and moved to Ontario during World War II where the father of the family served in the Dutch army cooking for his beloved queen who was in Canada for safety reasons. We had a most happy and unforgettable visit. While there they took us to the tobacco fields and the treatment or curing stations. For the first time in our lives we saw tobacco growing, and we were still in Canada. Hardly believable! But seeing is believing in this case. The idea many Americans have about Canada is that it is a cold, bleak, wasteland of snow and ice. More Americans should go there for their vacations, especially in the summer.

Our next stop was at Niagara Falls, although our honeymoon was twenty years gone. Niagara Falls truly is one of God's great wonder works. We, of course, were now in New York State and not very far away lived a pastor and family we had learned to know and love in Saskatchewan.

We made a short visit at their home. They lived in vineyard country. A number of his members had large vineyards. The pastor took us to see them and we ended up getting a bushel of grapes to take home with us. A new grape was being developed at the time. It was a beautiful red grape. A few bunches of these beautiful red grapes were laid on the top of our bushel of blue grapes. Gratefully we accepted them and were on our way again.

The next stop was in Faribault, Minnesota where our oldest daughter was teaching in Trinity Lutheran Parochial Grade School. After a few days of visiting between classes with our "schoolmarm" daughter, we were on our way again to make our next stop in Lloydminster. But as we crossed the Canadian line, the custom's officer had us worried about the bushel of grapes. We really were not to take certain fruits into the country. But after explaining to him how we got them, that we were not going to sell them but use all of them within our family, and after giving him a few bunches of the grapes, especially of the red grapes which he was admiring and asking questions about, he closed the trunk of the car and wished us a safe trip home. And again God did bring us safely back to our girls and field of work in His kingdom.

Our oldest daughter one day said when she was nearing the day of her graduation from high school, "I am going to go to Concordia Teachers' College in Seward, Nebraska. I want to be a parochial schoolteacher." At that time we just could not see our way clear to send her that far away from home. Our finances could hardly stand that much drainage. (I was still driving secondhand cars at that time.) My wife tried to talk her out of it, saying, "But, Girl, that is a long ways from home. How will you get there? Train or bus will cost a lot. And you will not be able to come home for Christmas. And it costs much to go to college." "I'll get a job for after school hours and Saturdays. Go to school for a while, work a while. And for Christmas I'll go to Grandma's. (That was seventy-five miles away.) I don't care; I am going to Seward." She was set on going. So we worked out something to get her there. The good Lord always knows a way out and He never forsakes His children. He may let the waters get very deep at times, but He brings us safely to the goal we set, which is to do His work, serve in His kingdom, and glorify Him. How grateful we are to Him that He helped us fulfill her heart's desire that she might serve Him by teaching children the saving truth of God's word and lead the lambs of Jesus on the path to heaven. Teaching parochial school has been the joy of her life and still is even though she has a family of three boys and one girl. Years later she once asked me whether I knew why she was so determined to teach in a parochial school. I, of course, had no idea. She said that it was something I said in a sermon I preached.

Our second daughter, Vera May, had her mind set on becoming a physical therapist. We inquired where she might get this training and we learned that there were only a few universities where such training was given at that time and these were in the States and the cost was about five thousand dollars. That was out, and she understood. She then trained for a laboratory technician, which training she received in a hospital in Edmonton, Alberta.

My last trip in the snow was for a church service scheduled at Battleford on a Thursday. It was a beautiful morning at Lloydminster when I left home. The road was reasonably good.

But the weather changed by the time I was about forty miles from home. Clouds began drifting in, the wind began to blow a little, and the snow began "scooting" across the road. Another fifteen miles further and drifts began to form and it began snowing. As I continued, I noticed that there had been a blizzard in this part of the country several days ago. There were some fairly large drifts across the road which the highway department had plowed open. In these cuts through the drifts is where I was having my difficulties. The snow was swirling around in them so that I could not see clearly and these cuts were also beginning to fill in.

The weather was getting worse and the temperature was dropping. The old snowdrifts were higher than my new car by now. But I kept working my way through. I was to preach the saving Gospel to blood-bought sinners. How many times I was stuck I just do not remember, but I know it was more often than I cherished it. The new drifts in the cuts through the old drifts were toward the left side. Due to the swirling snow in these cuts, I could not see just where these new drifts were. Again and again these new drifts grabbed my left front wheel and "bang," I ran into the old drifts and was stuck! The right door was the only door I could get open to get out to shovel myself out. This business got rather monotonous. Oh, yes, I always had a shovel with me in winter and I still do in Iowa.

Stuck! Shovel! Stuck! Shovel! What else could I do? I would not leave my new car stuck in a drift! Nosirree! Stuck once more but I did no more shoveling. I heard a truck snorting somewhere behind me. I decided to wait. It was "impossible" to get by me. The cuts here were not wide enough for two cars to meet. He would have to pull me out if he wanted to get somewhere. He had a chain. He pulled me out. But I was ahead of him. He agreed to pull me out again if I got stuck again. He did. We came to a place where the wind had cleaned the highway. There was no snow at all on the road. About a hundred feet or a few more was the driveway of my member where I was to stop in for dinner and then take them along to the worship service which was to be held in the home of another member.

Only a few yards beyond my member's driveway another long drift began. We could hear a tractor. We waited. Here he came. Where he was going I don't remember. He informed us that we could not get through because the road was blocked for more than a mile. But the trucker who helped me get through had a load of cattle to get to the stockyard about ten or twelve miles away. I presume truck and tractor made it. I did not "hang around" to find out. I was cold. I shoveled the snow out of the driveway far enough to park my new Chevy off the road. This done, I took my club bag with books and gown and walked to my member's house about a quarter of a mile away on a bluff. Here I stayed.

The snow continued falling, the wind continued blowing, the temperature continued dropping. The next day the snow stopped falling but the wind continued blowing most of the day. The worship service was not held. The third day came — Saturday. Quiet but cold. I had to get home to Lloydminster so I could conduct the worship service there on Sunday morning. But how would I get home? Roads were still blocked. The train did not get through for a day or longer. We were five miles from the nearest railroad station, North Battleford, which was a railroad divisional point, was about fifteen miles away. I phoned there to find out about the train. I was informed that the train would leave for Lloydminster, "As I remember it," in about two hours. The snowplow would go ahead of it.

The next move was to try to get to the town five miles away so I could catch the train there. My good host and member hitched his horses to the bobsled and off we went. Oh, what tough going for the horses! The snow was deep. We were pushing snow ahead of the sled constantly. There were drifts so deep that the horses lunged to get through pulling the sled. Before we were a mile away the horses were "steaming" from sweat. We rested them. We had to find our way through a field. The road was packed with high drifts. After a few more tries, I persuaded my member to turn back. I said, "You will kill your horses and I do not want that on my conscience. And you have to come back. No, turn around and go back home." After a few more tries to get somewhere, driving back and forth to avoid the drifts, he did head back home. The trail we had made was nearly all covered again by drifting snow. There was more breeze in the open than on the bluff. I was glad and thankful to get back into the house. I was cold, especially my feet. The horses, I am sure, were glad too to get back into the warm barn.

When my member came into the house, I said to him. "I wonder if the train would stop for me just after it crosses the North Saskatchewan River. The bridge is at the end of your land. That would be the only chance for me to get home and preach the saving Truth of God to our people in Lloydminster tomorrow. Would you take me there?" He said he would.

I then phoned the depot in North Battleford again and asked whether the train had left for Lloydminster. It had not. So I asked whether the train would stop for me after it crossed the bridge. The station agent said, "You will have to ask the conductor." I said, "Please get him to the phone." He did. I explained to him who I was and why I was so anxious to get home. I also told him that if I was standing next to the railroad near the bridge, I would appreciate it if he would have the train stop so I could get on it. He said, "You will have to talk to the engineer about that." I asked him to call the engineer to the phone. He did not but asked the engineer himself. He returned to the phone and told me that the engineer said that I should stand on the right side of the track — right side as the train was heading, wave my hands after the train had crossed the bridge, he would toot his whistle twice for a signal that he saw me, and then he would stop for me. He also informed me what time he would be there.

In the meantime, my hostess had a cup of coffee and a snack ready for us. Before long we were on our way through my member's field. Again the horses had to work hard to get through. We arrived at the place in ample time. We stayed in the sled out of the cold breeze. We looked to the hills from where my train would come to carry me home every few minutes — which seemed more like hours. The umpteenth time we looked, we spied it. I then made my own tracks in the snow to the railroad track. But there was a huge wire fence I had to get over before getting to the track. I made it over the fence all right, but on the other side was a ditch filled with snow into which I sank up to my chest and then I really had to struggle to make it with a heavy club bag of books and gown in my hand. I was frightened for a little while. I made it, but only because there is a greater Power always at hand to help us if we but ask and trust Him.

I got to the right side of the track, cleaned off the snow that had clung to my clothes and overcoat. The train was on the bridge and as soon as it had come around the bend, I waved my hands, the thing said "toot, toot," and stopped so that I did not have to walk more than one step to get on. "Service superduper!" The train moved on. About three hours later: home! Once again God kept His promise: "I will be with you always."

When our new Chevy was about ten months old, a letter arrived from the States containing a call from Zion congregation near Omaha, Nebraska. A decision had to be made. After 21 years in a country where we were not citizens, our girls likewise until they were of age and would vote, the church having been built, the congregation well established, the traveling, especially in the cold, becoming more and more difficult, I had to decide: is God calling me back to my homeland and a warmer climate or had I accomplished what God sent me to do for Him in Canada? I presented the call to the congregation and also to the preaching stations, gave them my reasons why I was inclined to accept the call, and asked them for their advice and their prayers. Some had expressed their desire that I decline the call, some were neutral, but most of them were truly understanding, saying that in one congregation and being a country congregation in a milder climate and with less traveling, the work load probably would be a little lighter, and even though they would like to have me stay, they would not, however, accuse me of forsaking them if I did accept the call.

After a few more weeks of prayer and thinking and discussion with my family, I decided to accept the call and to terminate my work in the Lloydminster parish on the third Sunday in September. This gave me almost a month to complete certain work I had started and thus leave no loose strings dangling. The District Board of Missions also was notified in plenty of time so they could appoint a new circuit counselor in my place and also take my name off the "missionary pay list."

There was one person, a young man, who wanted very much that I instruct and confirm him in the Christian faith before I leave. I agreed to do this, and did it, and he became a most faithful member and still is.

A busy month was ahead of us to get the furniture, pots and pans, and a hundred other small and big things, including my 12 gauge shotgun, sold. Fortunately there was a community auction in town the last week of our stay in town. My good wife took what we had not sold over there. There was also the packing and crating of books and bedding, some dishes, and a few more things besides personal "keepsake" things to pack. And the car had to be sold and that is a story all in itself which I will tell a little later. The worst of all, while the "mad rush" was on, I landed in the hospital with bronchial pneumonia, thus leaving all the work for my wife and girls to do. By the time I got out of the hospital, my right thigh looked like a pincushion from the penicillin shots I got every three hours day and night. But the good Lord restored me to health and allowed me to finish my work.

It was necessary that letters be written to Zion Lutheran congregation in Nebraska regarding shipment of our things. Tickets for our journey by train had to be bought. A declaration of contents of the boxes to be shipped had to be made in writing and I had to deal and dicker with the man who wanted to buy our "new" Chevy. It was almost at the point that I was going in circles. Farewell sermons had to be written and they are not easy ones to write. I know one thing for sure — I did not need a diet to lose weight during this last month in Lloydminster.

We had everything well under control by the Sunday of my farewell service. Our date set for boarding the train was the 13th day of September, 1951 — not Friday the 13th but Thursday the 13th. Yet it almost brought "bad luck" anyway. The man wanting to buy my car did not let himself be heard from. I was getting on "edge" over this. I still had to exchange the Canadian money I was to receive from him into American money. It was Wednesday. I phoned him again. He told me he would be at my house by noon. It was after noon and he did not come. What should I do? I finally went to the bank and told the banker my predicament. He was not surprised that the man had not shown himself. The banker told me: "The bank closes at three o'clock. After you have closed the deal, even if it is after three, you come here, knock on the door, and I will take care of you." It was after three when the man finally came to close the deal. The banker cheerfully and in good Canadian-style courtesy took care of my needs and gave me a bank draft in American money. What a relief! So we could say: "All is well that ends well."

I just cannot remember where or how we spent our last night in Lloydminster. But I do remember that the family, except the oldest daughter who was teaching parochial school in Faribault, Minnesota, was at the railroad depot in good time. The boxes were sent by freight the day before.

The train arrived. Some members of the congregation were there to see us off and to wish as God's blessings. We boarded the train with great excitement and yet with a peculiar tugging feeling in our hearts and our eyes just a little blurry. But we could say with definiteness and gratitude: God had been undeservedly good to us in the twenty-one years we spent in the ministry of the Lord which I hope and trust I have clearly given witness to in this book I have written telling about my ministry in Canada "As I Remember It."

GLORY BE TO GOD, Father, Son,
And Holy Spirit, Three in One,
As 'twas, is now, and so shall be
world without end, eternally!

Made in the USA
Coppell, TX
12 January 2024

27616593R00079